S0-ACF-095

The Woman's Guide to Gambling

Other Books by John Scarne

SKARNEY—Rules for 10 Terrific New Card Games
The Odds Against Me
Scarne's Complete Guide to Gambling
The Amazing World of John Scarne
Scarne on Teeko
Scarne's Magic Tricks
Scarne on Card Tricks
Scarne on Cards
Scarne on Dice

The Woman's Guide to Gambling

John Scarne

CROWN PUBLISHERS, INC., NEW YORK

All Rights Reserved
Including the Right of Reproduction
In Whole or in Part in Any Form
Copyright © 1967 by John Scarne Games, Inc.
Library of Congress Catalog Card Number: 67–27036
Published by Crown Publishers, Inc.
419 Park Avenue South
New York, N.Y. 10016
Printed in the U.S.A.

Second Printing, April, 1968

This book is dedicated to the
48 million women gamblers who
are trying to beat the odds

CONTENTS

Publisher's Note About the Author   ix

1   America's Panorama of Women
    Gamblers   1

2   Gambling Primer for Women   13

3   Bank Craps   29

4   Blackjack, B.J., or Twenty-one   54

5   Roulette   71

6   Slot Machines   86

7   Bingo   94

8   Keno—Nevada Style   102

9   The Numbers Game   107

10   Lotteries   114

11   Betting on the Horses   124

12   How to Win at Gin Rummy   144

13   How to Win at Poker   152

14   Protection Against Card Cheats   164

Publisher's Note About the Author

To most readers of this book John Scarne needs no introduction. But a good book travels far, lives long, and reaches many people. So, for the sake of those to whom John Scarne is just a name, here are some facts.

John Scarne is the world's leading card manipulator, and stands alone as the outstanding gambling authority in the world today. He is also the inventor of Skarney, history's most exciting card game, and the skill-board games of Teeko, Follow-the-Arrow, and Scarney (not to be confused with the card game).

He is the author of many popular books on magic, games, and gambling, including the best seller *Scarne's Complete Guide to Gambling* and the standard reference books on card and dice games, *Scarne on Cards* and *Scarne on Dice*.

Scarne's revised rules of play in card and dice games have made the phrase "according to Hoyle" obsolete. Millions of players from Las Vegas to Puerto Rico to Monte Carlo now say, "according to Scarne."

Mr. Scarne's fame as the top authority on games of skill and chance dates from World War II, when he acted as gambling adviser to the United States Armed Forces. During World War II he gave hundreds of lectures on gambling before thousands of members of the Armed Forces, to teach them how to avoid being cheated by crooked gamblers.

Scarne has also been called into consultation as an expert on games and gambling by the United States Senate, the Federal Bureau of Investigation, the British Home Office, the Puerto Rican Government, the Government of Panama, the Hilton International Company hotel chain, and numerous other government and hotel agencies throughout the world.

1

America's Panorama of Women Gamblers

In 1960, I completed a five-year nationwide survey of all kinds of gambling in the United States. The findings of this survey first appeared in print in my 714-page best seller *Scarne's Complete Guide to Gambling*, and revealed that in 1960, 70 percent of our adult population—almost 86 million Americans, of whom 46 million were women and 40 million were men—paid the astronomical sum of $50 billion for their legal and illegal gambling pleasure. Women gamblers contributed $15 billion; male gamblers, $35 billion.

On August 22, 1961, the findings of this survey were requested, received, and used by Senator John McClellan, Chairman of the United States Senate Permanent Subcommittee on Investigations, and later by the Attorney General's office and several other branches of the Federal Government.

It wasn't long after my survey findings were made public that I began to notice a great upsurge in the number of women casino gamblers in Las Vegas and Puerto Rican gambling casinos. At the Caribe Hilton Hotel Casino in San Juan, Puerto

Rico, where I have been (and still am) overseer for Conrad Hilton for the past fifteen years, I very often clocked a greater number of women gambling than men. The only casino game where women gamblers were outnumbered by men was at the dice tables.

What amazed me was the way most of these women gambled—they were actually throwing their money away. In the parlance of the professional gambler, they were and still are "rank suckers."

This situation reminded me of a similar situation that confronted me during World War II when as gambling consultant to the United States Armed Forces I was called upon to help reduce the sucker population among 12 million servicemen. At that time most GI's were so naïve when it came to gambling that at certain games there were times when they would accept even-money bets when they should be getting odds of 2 to 1 or better.

In an effort to lessen this sucker situation among women gamblers, I decided to write a book for them—in language they would understand—and at the same time undertake another gambling survey—a study of America's women gamblers.

I wanted to learn, among other things, facts and figures on women gamblers, how many women were now gambling, why they gambled and what kind of gambling they preferred, what got them started, and what they knew about the game they favored; but, more important, what they did not know and should know.

To avoid any bias in these results, I knew I had to interview a random sample of the population. For this reason, I carefully avoided questioning anyone I saw gambling, and I did not include anyone I knew in advance to be a gambler.

My survey covered a two-year period from January, 1965, to December, 1966. Aided by several assistants, I obtained replies from 20,000 women and 20,000 men.

Other survey questions were designed to obtain many facts and figures that concern the professional gambling operator. I questioned countless legal and illegal gambling-house operators, scores of operators of Bingo parlors, and dozens of racetrack and carnival owners. In addition, I studied the findings of my previous five-year nationwide gambling survey and the numerous gambling reports issued by various state agencies that permit legalized gambling in one form or another.

The findings of this survey revealed that in 1966, 73 percent of our adult population—almost 90 million Americans, of whom 48 million were women and 42 million were men—paid the astronomical sum of $50 billion for their legal and illegal gambling pleasure. Women contributed $16 billion and male gamblers, $34 billion.

Among the nation's 48 million women gamblers, some 2½ million women earn their living, or part of it, from gambling. They include gambling operators and their employees, private-game hustlers, hookers, steerers, and cheats.

My male questionnaire consisted of just one question, "Do you gamble?"

"Yes," was the reply given by 67 percent of the 20,000 men questioned.

My woman's questionnaire included, among many others, such questions as: "Do you gamble?" "What is your favorite gambling activity?" "Why do you gamble?" "When did you first start gambling?" "Do you know why you lose more often than you win?" "Have you read any books on gambling?" "If you don't gamble, why not?"

Answers were obtained from women in all walks of life, and in varied urban and rural areas throughout the United States.

Most women I approached were interested in the subject and in the questions, and were eager to supply the answers. Some required a little persuasion before putting themselves on record, and a few said, in no uncertain terms: "I'm not interested in your survey. I'm busy."

Here are my findings from the questions above:

1. Do you gamble?—"Yes," was the answer given by 78 percent of the women. However, 5 percent of this group who answered "Yes" stated that in addition they earned their living (or part of it) from gambling by being associated with some legal or illegal gambling operation.

2. What is your favorite gambling activity?—The replies

listed below show the gambling activities favored by most women in order of number of participants:

First: Gambling at cards.

The four most popular card games favored by a vast majority of women card players (in order of number of players) are: (1) Poker, (2) Rummy, (3) Bridge, and (4) Pinochle.

Second: Gambling at lotteries, sweepstakes, and pools.

Third: Gambling at Bingo, Numbers, Keno, and similar games.

Fourth: Gambling at the racetrack and with off-track bookies.

Fifth: Gambling in casinos and gaming rooms.

The five most popular gambling-house games favored by women gamblers, in order of the number of participants, are as follows: (1) Slot Machines, (2) Blackjack, (3) Roulette, (4) Bank Craps, (5) casino side games that include wheels of fortune and various other games.

Sixth: Gambling at carnival, bazaar, and amusement-park games of skill and chance.

The vast majority stated that they did not confine themselves to the one form of gambling they listed as their favorite, but also indulged in one or more kinds of gambling pursuits.

3. Why do you gamble?—The majority, 55 percent, replied that they gamble primarily to win money. Forty percent replied that they gamble for pleasure and the excitement that it affords. The remaining 5 percent gamble for reasons that have nothing to do with gambling itself: a woman goes to racetracks with her husband and friends just to have something to do; a lady casino gambler plays the "one-armed bandits" (slot machines) to pass the time away while waiting for her husband to leave the dice or blackjack table.

4. When did you first start gambling?—Half of this group replied that they first started gambling for pennies at an early age when playing cards with their parents; 30 percent said they first started to gamble at Bingo and at Canasta or Bridge; 10 percent stated that they first started to gamble during a visit to a racetrack; and the remaining 10 percent blamed their hus-

bands, boyfriends, and acquaintances for inducing them to make their first wager.

5. Do you know why you lose more often than you win?— Half of this group said that they knew that the operator's percentage beats them in the long run, but that they can't figure it and don't know how it works against them; 20 percent answered that they were unlucky and that was why they lost most of the time; 15 percent said that they were still a little green about gambling and that was why they lost most of the time; and the remaining 15 percent gave assorted reasons, such as the woman who replied, "Gambling is crooked—that goes for casinos, racing, Bingo, and all the rest"; the woman who said, "The reason I lose at Poker and most other card games is that I don't have card sense"; or the woman who replied, "I never lose. I run the game."

6. Have you read any books on gambling?—The majority, 70 percent, replied, "No." Another 25 percent said they glanced through a number of gambling books but couldn't become interested because they seemed so complicated. Four percent said that after reading their husband's or a friend's book on gambling, and learning that the operators' cut at their favorite gambling activity was unreasonably high, they decided to switch to a game that gave them a better percentage break. The remaining 1 percent said that they have purchased and read a number of gambling books but that doing so didn't help them any: they still lose.

7. If you don't gamble, why not?—Half of this group said that they used to gamble but that they stopped because they couldn't control their gambling emotions; 40 percent said they could not afford it; 5 percent said they knew nothing about gambling; 3 percent stated that they believed all forms of gambling are sinful; and the remaining 2 percent gave assorted reasons, such as the young lady who said: "My boyfriend threatens to break our engagement if he catches me gambling. I want to marry him, so I don't gamble."

An analysis of the sample findings of my 1965–1966 nationwide women's gambling survey states that the annual gambling "handle" on all forms of gambling in the United States had reached the gigantic sum of $500 billion, only $25 billion legally. How does this $500 billion figure compare with that of 1960? My previous five-year survey revealed a similar $500 billion figure for 1960, except that only $10 billion was wagered legally compared to $25 billion during 1966.

In the past five years, owing to the legislation of Bingo, raffles, and lotteries in some states, in addition to the sharp increase in the nation's racing handle and other lawful forms of gambling, the legal betting handle in America jumped from $10 billion in 1960 to $25 billion in 1966.

This is ample proof that legalized gambling is on the march in the United States.

Note that this annual $500 billion gambling handle is not the sum won or lost by America's 90 million gamblers in 1966; it is the betting handle, which is something entirely different—it is the total amount wagered. Most of these $500 billion dollars are counted many times because they are bet back and forth many times during the year between players, and between players and gambling operators, before they are finally won or lost.

For example, the 100-odd Nevada gambling establishments grossed (won) $300 million last year, an increase of $100 million over 1960. After clocking the five most popular casino games in Las Vegas and elsewhere, I have found that, on the average, four cents out of each dollar wagered is retained by the house. If the $300 million is 4 percent, then the gross betting handle for legalized gambling in Nevada in 1966 comes to $7½ billion. From this $500 billion gigantic betting handle for 1966, the actual cost to the millions of losers for their year's gambling pleasure at professionally and privately operated gambling games amounts to about 10 percent, or $50 billion. Women gamblers paid $16 billion and male gamblers $34 billion.

An analysis of the findings of organized gambling shows that professional operators retained $37 billion of the $50 billion total paid by 90 million Americans for the pleasure they received from organized forms of gambling. Women spent (or lost, if you want to look at it that way) $12 billion; men spent $25 billion.

Organized gambling includes: lotteries, raffles, pools, Bingo, Keno, Numbers, betting at racetracks, with race and sports bookies, in gambling establishments that harbor dice and card games, slot machines, Roulette, wheels of fortune, gambling at carnivals, bazaars, amusement parks, games of skill and chance, and so on.

My survey of private gambling gives me reason to estimate that in 1966, about $13 billion was lost among friends, acquaintances, and strangers; and of this amount women who lost contributed about $4 billion, men about $9 billion. Private gambling includes games played among friends, acquaintances, and strangers at all kinds of card games (Poker, Gin, Blackjack, Pinochle, Bridge, and so on), at Craps and other dice games, at guessing games, sports, elections, and other forms of gambling, mostly of an illegal nature, in which a professional operator or banker does not profit.

Why is America's womanhood now experiencing its greatest gambling boom in history? The reasons I give below are based not only on the results of my women's gambling survey but also on a lifetime of observation and study of every facet of gambling.

1. The enormous fascination that Bingo holds over women was responsible for a totally unexpected new breed of women gamblers. Millions of elderly and middle-aged women, many of whom previously frowned on all forms of gambling, and regarded every gambler as a bad character or criminal, visited a Bingo parlor for the first time. Once there, they began playing, liked it—and soon became Bingo fanatics. Bingo, with its 20 million women players and only 1 million male players, is by far the principal reason why America's women gamblers outnumbered their male counterparts by 6 million.*

---

* The above Bingo figures, when compared to those of my 1960 survey, show an increase of 3 million women players and a decrease of 3 million male players during the past five years.

2. Legalization in some states of horse racing, greyhound racing, casino games, Bingo, Poker, lotteries, raffles, carnival games, and slot machines has created new opportunities for gambling legally. The fact that these operations are legal and under state supervision gives assurance to players that they can gamble to their hearts' content without fear of arrest; and because of this, millions of women who did not gamble before now do so. Once they become confirmed gamblers, they seek action wherever they can find it, whether it is legal or not.

3. A great many women have more money today than ever before, and for the first time can afford to gamble.

4. The daily publicity that the nation's newspapers give to horse racing—their listings and daily entries, results, payoff mutuels, raters' and handicappers' selections—have induced millions of women who never before bet on a horse race to visit the tracks. Once there, they begin betting and become horse bettors. Once the horse-betting bug has bitten them, they place race bets not only at the track but also with their local bookies.

5. The deluge of newspaper, radio, and television publicity about the first lottery run in the United States in decades—the "New Hampshire State Lottery"—induced millions of women to purchase these and other lottery and raffle tickets in the United States.

6. The enormous popularity of Canasta and Bridge in recent years created millions of women card players, most of whom began for the first time to play for money. Because any card game eventually loses interest when little or no financial stake is involved, many also began to gamble at simpler and faster games, such as Poker, Gin Rummy, Blackjack, and so on.

7. Since gambling was first legalized in Nevada in 1931, the constant publicity given to its numerous multimillion-dollar hotel casinos and its live entertainment, which is unmatched anywhere in the world, has attracted tens of millions of women tourists to Las Vegas—women who previously knew little or nothing about casino games. While there, they visited the casinos, learned to play Roulette, Blackjack, Craps, the wheels

of fortune, slot machines, and other casino games. Because they enjoyed them, when they returned home they looked for action in other gambling establishments.

There are seven different kinds of women gamblers. Which kind are you?

1. The occasional woman gambler who knows little or nothing about the hard mathematical and psychological facts of the games on which she now and then wagers some money. The vast majority of America's women gamblers fall into this class.

2. The habitual, or degenerate, woman gambler who plays constantly and knows a great deal about gambling but is not smart enough to know that she can't beat adverse odds. She craves action, any kind of action, and she lives in a dream world in which she hopes someday to make a big killing and then quit gambling forever. However, when she does make a big winning, she almost always gambles it all back, and, like most gamblers, ends by being a loser.

3. The skilled or experienced woman gambler who knows much more about any sort of gambling than the occasional or habitual woman gambler, plays a much better game than they do, and consequently wins more often than she loses. She is usually on hand to start the game; she specializes in private games mostly patronized by women; and favors such games as Poker, Gin Rummy, Blackjack, Craps, and so on. This woman plays for blood; she seldom gives another player a break because she believes that is no way to earn money at gambling. She usually knows better than most women where the favorable percentage lies in most private games of chance, such as Craps, and she makes the most of this by offering the occasional and habitual women gamblers sucker odds, which they, not knowing any better, usually accept.

4. The professional woman gambler or gambling operator who earns her living (or most of it) by operating some gambling scheme. She is called a gambler because she runs a gambling operation, but she really doesn't gamble. She is a businesswoman who runs a gambling operation and understands her trade, and either makes direct levies on the play or receives a

percentage because the odds are in her favor. The professional woman gambler, like the legitimate broker, charges a commission for her services in accepting wagers. She is not betting against the players; they are actually betting against one another. Her employees are also in this category.

5. The woman gambling cheat or crook who makes money by cheating at cards or dice, operating a fixed carnival game or other gaffed (crooked) gambling device. Also included in this category are many women employees of a crooked gambling house or any participants in a crooked scheme, whether or not they do the actual cheating themselves. Included in this group are the many lady steerers who secretly work for card or dice cheats and lure male gamblers to a crooked game. The cheat's gamble is not so much in winning or losing as in whether or not she will get away with it.

6. The woman gambling hooker and woman gambling hustler. The hooker knows that the only way to beat the game is by gambling with someone else's money, and she usually gets it by inducing a male sponsor at a racetrack or gambling casino to give or lend her money with which to gamble. She usually bets only a part of the money, and pockets the rest; if she wins, she usually keeps it all—if she loses it all, she loses nothing.

In a poker game the woman hustler often forgets to put up her ante at her turn of play, and she is quick to grab any sleepers (money belonging to another player that the latter has forgotten about). She will borrow money during a private game, and forget about paying it back.

The woman gambling hustler—and there are many such— preys mostly on the habitual, chronic women gamblers. She is often caught, but that doesn't deter her, since she considers it an occupational hazard.

7. The woman system player who lives in a dream world all her own, believing that it is only a question of time until she finds an infallible betting system with which she can amass a fortune. She is a perfect mark (sucker) for racetrack touts. She buys tips and most of the advertised systems; and although they fail, one after another, she buys more, always hoping to find the

one that is perfect. The racetrack or casino woman system player always carries a small pad on which she is eternally making calculations.

It is a sad commentary that one of the country's biggest businesses is conducted mostly outside the law. Only one of the fifty states, Nevada, legally permits casino and off-track betting. There are twenty-five states in which pari-mutuel betting at the tracks is legal; seven permit betting on dog races; twelve have legalized Bingo and raffles; four allow slot-machine operations in varying degrees of activity; Nevada and California permit gambling at Poker; and one, New Jersey, permits the operation of carnival games. New Hampshire and New York have the only legal lottery operations in the United States.

Believe me, of the thousands and thousands of women gamblers whose play I studied during my career in gambling casinos, carnivals, Bingo parlors, racetracks, and so on, I have found that only one out of a hundred has the vaguest idea about the operator's percentage they must overcome to win. Lack of such vital statistics reduces their chances of winning— over a prolonged period—to exactly zero.

At the swank Caribe Hilton Hotel Casino in San Juan, Puerto Rico, whence I have been commuting for the past fifteen years, hundreds of women gamblers have approached me at one time or another and asked, "Mr. Scarne, will you please teach me how to play this game so I can win occasionally?"

My answer usually runs as follows: "Buy my gambling books. All the information you need to better your chances of winning can be found in my books."

The reply most often given was, "Mr. Scarne, I have glanced through several of your books, but they are too big and complicated for me to understand."

Remarks such as these first started me thinking about writing a gambling book that women would read and could easily understand.

In concluding this chapter, I should like to emphasize that gambling when indulged in moderately is not harmful—but there is no question that it is harmful when carried to excess, just as drinking, smoking, or eating is harmful when carried to excess. However, I want to point out that this book, the first of its kind—for women gamblers—was not written to encourage women to gamble. You will see as you read that it does just the opposite. The more a woman knows about the basic principles of gambling, the less chance she has of becoming a habitual gambler. I firmly believe that this book (if read by enough women gamblers) will greatly reduce the number of women gambling suckers in the United States.

I also believe that just as a woman increases the pleasure and satisfaction that she gets out of fine music and literature by studying their underlying principles, so can she increase the pleasure and satisfaction that she derives out of gambling by studying its fundamental principles, which are thoroughly explained in the following pages.

This book explains the most common faults of women players in all forms of gambling. It explains how to gamble sensibly; it gives the woman gambler the best bet and the adverse odds or percentages she must buck at her favorite gambling pastime, as well as many tips on how to avoid being fleeced by gambling cheats. It explains in detail the "Scarne Shuffle" and the "Scarne Cut," a shuffle and cut I invented during World War II as a defensive weapon against card sharks for the millions of men in the Armed Forces. Today, untold millions of card players the world over—including James Bond, the fabulous 007— make use of both these anticheating defensive weapons when gambling at cards. It also gives Scarne's system of betting the races, Blackjack, Bank Craps, Poker, Gin Rummy, and other games favored by women gamblers.

Here, for the first time, you will find several full-page illustrations depicting the best bets, payoff odds, and percentages at various casino games. This and other information have never before appeared in print. They afford a quick, handy reference to all the best bets at your favorite gambling pastime.

In this book you will also find strong evidence to prove that gambling against adverse odds is not one of the most trustworthy methods for reaching and living on Easy Street.

2

Gambling Primer
for Women

If you are one of the 48 million American women who gamble at racetracks, Bingo halls, gambling casinos, poker rooms, play the Numbers game, buy lottery tickets, or bet with race and sports bookies, remember that you must pay for your pleasure.

That is not unreasonable. You expect to pay for a Broadway show, so why not for your gambling pleasure? Moreover, someone has to pay the gambling operators' expenses. The gambling operator charges a commission for every bet he accepts. It is a business like any other; and if the operators did not wind up with a handsome yearly net profit, you would not have a place in which to gamble.

How much you pay for this entertainment is entirely up to you. If you are one of the millions of women gambling suckers, who know little or nothing about gambling, I guarantee the price you are paying is much more than you ever imagined. My gambling survey revealed that the amateurish betting habits of most of the 48 million women gamblers greatly reduce their winning chances. The experienced male gambler has a much better chance of winning.

There are a dozen or more well-known big-time men gamblers who win too consistently, and are barred from playing at the gaming tables in most Nevada casinos. When you ask a casino operator the reason, he says: "These players are too tough to beat. When we beat them we win small; when they beat us they win big."

The mathematicians and the gambling writers I read say, "If you gamble against adverse odds, over the long run you must lose."

This is good advice, except that it doesn't apply to most of the 48 million American women gamblers today because they don't gamble that much or that long. They are occasional gamblers, many of whom gamble only a few times a year. Not all of them lose; a few win, and many more *should* win.

Now, what constitutes a long run?

A long run for an occasional woman gambler may consist of the total number of bets she makes in a lifetime. To the habitual woman gambler it may be the number of bets she makes in a week or a month; and to the operators who accept wagers from hundreds of players daily, a long run may consist of the total number of bets made against him in a single day or night.

If all players always lost, gambling operators would have folded up long ago. The advice "Don't gamble; you can't win," is not true for every gambler all the time. There are thousands of gamblers who have won—and thousands more who will win—thousands of dollars gambling.

The author personally knows a woman who won $250,000 at the dice tables in Las Vegas in a three-month period of play, and a woman who won $200,000 in six weeks of play at several Havana baccarat tables before Fidel Castro came to power.

Indisputable proof that some people do win is seen in the announcement of the $56,000 and $140,000 winners in the world's best known lottery, the Irish Hospitals' Sweepstakes.

It is true, of course, that the majority of women gamblers lose. It is doubly true that they lose more often than they should because they know little or nothing about gambling. With the exception of the 5 percent who earn their living or part of it from gambling, women gamblers today are making fools of themselves by contributing billions of dollars annually to legal and illegal gambling operators here and abroad.

Most women gamblers I interviewed during my survey know that the operator has an advantage over the players, but it doesn't keep the players away from betting. Each woman believes that there is no reason why, if she hits a lucky streak, she should not win money. Even when they lose, they return again and again, as long as their bankrolls hold out. Why? Primarily it is the human desire to win; second, it's the glamour and excitement of gambling.

My survey also revealed that most women gamblers, like men gamblers, forget the times they lose, and remember only the times they win.

I can't tell you how to beat a raffle or a lottery, but if you frequent gambling casinos I can tell you how to bet your money, and make you as gambling wise as the top male professional gamblers in Las Vegas and Reno. And who knows? Perhaps in the near future you'll become such a consistent winner that you'll become the first woman gambler to be barred from playing at the gaming tables in Nevada. However, I must warn you that the gambling casino, racetrack, or Bingo parlor is one place where you will never find a game of skill. Such places make money because at no organized gambling scheme can your skill be of any real help to you. Knowledge of the odds can be a real help, but that is not skill. It is knowledge.

But let's try to define our terms; let's see what we're talking about.

What is gambling?

Gambling consists of wagering money upon the outcome of any event or game of chance or skill or game that combines both chance and skill. A game of skill is a game from which the element of chance has been utterly eliminated. Examples are Chess, Checkers, and three skill games that I invented myself: Teeko, Follow-the-Arrow, and the game Scarney—each of which has already been hailed by millions of devotees to be one of the most fascinating, educational, and strategic skill games on the market today. If you and your family happen to like skill games, you will love these. In them, the skilled player will invariably win against an unskilled opponent, and the skilled woman's winning advantage will be an exact reflection of the relation between her ability and that of a less skilled opponent.

In private card games, such as Poker, Gin Rummy, or Bridge, that combine skill and chance, the more skilled player enjoys an advantage over the player with less skill.

A game of chance is a game from which the element of skill has been utterly eliminated. All organized gambling ventures are basically games of chance. These include: betting at the racetrack or with your local bookies, Bingo, lotteries, raffles, sports pools, Numbers, and all gambling-casino games such as slot machines, Bank Craps, Blackjack, Roulette, wheels of fortune, and all other games found therein. It is true that special knowledge about the horses in a race, or about players in a game of football, basketball, and so on, can be helpful. But that is not skill as I mean it. It is knowledge.

Now, what is chance? How does it work?

Forgive me if I sound pedantic, but I believe that gambling should be taught, along with the three R's, in every elementary school. If it were so taught, gambling would be reduced from a national problem to a sporadic eccentricity, and most games of chance would fall by the wayside. With a very few dangerous exceptions, the average educated woman has no knowledge of gambling, and very little interest in it; this ignorance costs average educated women gamblers in the United States hundreds of millions of dollars a year.

There is a branch of mathematics called the theory of probability. It is called by gamblers—erroneously—the law of averages. Probability theory offers mathematical methods for discovering what can be expected to happen when the results depend upon chance. It states, for instance, that each player in a game of chance has about an equal chance to win in the long run. If, during a long evening of play at Poker or Bridge, you never get a decent hand, or when you do get a fairly decent hand someone else always gets a better one, you may doubt this. But your experience does not contradict the theory of probability, because the theory does not pretend to state that you and the other players will get an equal number of good hands in one evening of play. It states that the longer you play, the more likely you are to get approximately the same number of good hands.

Be careful that you don't misunderstand that last statement. Probability theory says, for instance, that when you toss a coin, heads will turn up *about* half the time in the long run. It doesn't say that in a very long run, heads and tails *must* come up exactly the same *number* of times.

Coin-tossing experiments have shown that the deviation between the actual numerical results and the expected results sometimes increases in long runs. In a series of 100 tosses you may get 45 heads or 55 heads instead of the expected 50, a deviation of 5 heads from the expectation. In a series of 10,000 tosses, the difference between the actual result and the expected result may have increased to 50 over or under the expected 5,000.

But consider the deviation from the percentage standpoint. In a series of 100 tosses, the difference of 5 heads over or under the expected 50 is 10 percent. In a series of 10,000 tosses, the difference of 50 heads from the expected 5,000 is only 1 percent. The percentage of difference does tend to decrease in the long run. It is only in this sense that results tend to "even up."

But as far as we're concerned, the theory of probability affords a method of calculating what can be expected to happen in a situation in which some of the factors are not at hand or, being at hand, are too complex to be easily broken down, assimilated, and used.

When you double the insurance on your car, you are both

gambling and making use of the theory of probability. The whole gigantic life-insurance business is based on the actuarial mortality tables, which are just a list of probabilities. Any businesswoman drafting a budget or schedule or sales program is applying a theory of probabilities. The theory holds rigorously true for racetracks, race and sports bookies, Bingo parlors, the Numbers game, and other games of chance. For example, let's take the game of Bank Craps, the game that gets the most action in Las Vegas casinos. Each dice shooter, the theory goes, will in the long run have an approximately equal number of hot and cold hands.

"Malarkey, Scarne," you say, "there are times when for hours I stand at the dice table betting the dice to pass, and I don't win a bet. Then I try the Blackjack table, and I can't pick up a winning hand there. In short, I lose at whatever game I play."

You're right. But, it's not "malarkey, Scarne," it's the theory of probabilities. Like Roulette or wheels of fortune, dice or cards don't, and mustn't be expected to, behave exactly according to probabilities. But sooner or later they'll come awfully close.

Toss a coin. It may fall heads up ten times in a row. Then it may fall tails up ten times in a row. And there are women gamblers who, after heads have been turned on several successive tosses, will double their bet that it will fall tails up next. They think the odds, or probabilities, favor tails. Similarly, most women casino gamblers operate on the belief that, after they have lost four or five bets at Craps, Blackjack, or Roulette, the probabilities abruptly shift to favor their winning the next bet. Thereupon they raise the size of their bet on their next wager, and are shocked and saddened when they lose.

There is an old gambler's truism that applies here: "The Roulette ball has no eyes," which means that the ball can't see, smell, or think. It doesn't know where it dropped last or will drop next. The same thing applies to dice, cards, slot machines, and wheels of fortune.

This notion that luck has a cumulative tendency to change

is known academically as the doctrine of the maturity of chances. Mathematicians for years have referred to it as the "gamblers' fallacy," but 99 percent of all women gamblers, many of them brilliantly educated persons, go right on believing in it and losing their money on it.

The theory of probability is not that a player will hit a winning streak after suffering a losing streak. It is that in the long run her winning and losing streaks are expected to be just like anybody else's—which is something very different. How a player handles her money when a winning or losing streak takes place does not enter into this discussion—at least not at present.

"Very well, then," I think you may be saying, "I've seen players much luckier than I am. They always seem to be around when the dice are hot. I'm sure they have had more winning nights than me. Now, what?"

You raised the question: What is luck?

Well, my dictionary defines luck as "that which happens to a person as if by chance, a person's apparent tendency to be fortunate or unfortunate."

The key word in that definition is "apparent." Anyone who believes that one player has a better chance of winning a bet because she is luckier than another is no smarter than the followers of the sorcerers and witches of the Middle Ages or those of the African voodoo doctor or the gypsy fortuneteller who reads tea leaves. I agree wholeheartedly with my eleven-year-old son, John Teeko, when he says, "Luck is for the suckers."

If you gambled and won yesterday, you may correctly say that you were lucky, because you are merely stating that you placed your bets in such a way that they agreed with the horses that ran first in all nine races at Aqueduct or with the dice shooter who made ten straight passes at the Bank Craps table at the Caesars Palace in Las Vegas. But the fact that you were lucky yesterday, or that you have been consistently lucky in your affairs, does not guarantee you a better break than the next gal tomorrow. The odds on the races, dice, cards, Numbers, Roulette, Bingo, raffles, lotteries, or any other gambling scheme are not different for different people at different times. If your past luck has any effect on your future luck, then some supernatural force is working.

The supernatural will continue to get a foot in the door just as long as we try to investigate chance as it applies to a single person. But if we consider chance as it applies to a large group of players and a long series of wagers, then we begin to make sense, and superstition gets a quick brush-off.

One of the first things we discover is that the marvelous run of luck you had yesterday or last week isn't always so astonishing as it seems. At Roulette, the lady who puts her money on the single zero and takes 35 to 1 that it will win on the next spin of the wheel feels that she is a very lucky gal indeed when the single zero hits six times in a row, and she bets on each turn of the wheel, especially if she happens to know that the odds against such a thing are 1 in 133,448,704. She is amazed that some mysterious fate has singled her out for such a favor. But the gal who was betting the maximum limit on double zeros and lost six big bets when the single zero popped six times in succession would consider herself as being the champion hard-luck gal in the world, and as far as she is concerned that closes the subject.

As a matter of fact, it is just the threshold of the subject, for the odds are and will remain exactly the same for the single and double zeros. Over a number of such bets sufficient to let the probabilities get their teeth into the statistics, say 10,000 or 100,000 spins of the wheel, the percentage difference in single- and double-zero wins will be negligible. It is true in theory, it is true in the practice of many experimenters, and it is the truth on which gambling operators grow rich, since their income is based on the inexorable certainty that paying off winning bets at less than correct odds will never fail over the long run.

Now, what are odds? How do they work?

We cannot predict whether heads or tails will be thrown on the next toss of a coin, but since heads can be expected to come half the time, we can say that its chance of appearing is $\frac{1}{2}$, or that it has a probability of ½. With a symmetrical die of six sides, each side has an equal chance with each of the others, and we can expect any one side to be thrown an average of once in six times. Its probability is ⅙.

With two dice, each of the six sides of one die can be combined with each of the six sides of the other to form 6×6, or 36, combinations. The chance that any combination of two like numbers, such as two aces, two deuces, and so on will appear is 1 in 36, or $\frac{1}{36}$.

When an event has a probability of 0, it is an impossible event; when the probability is 1, the event is certain. All other probabilities are expressed by fractions falling between 0 and 1. When the probability is ½, we say the chances are fifty-fifty, or even. A probability of ⅙ is less than an even chance. The fraction is the mathematical way of saying an event has 1 chance of happening in a total of 6 possible chances.

We use the fraction when calculating probability problems, but for betting purposes we express the probability differently. We state it in terms of the advantage that the unfavorable chances have over the favorable chances, or in terms of the odds against the event's happening. Any specific side of a die has a probability of ⅙, and the odds against that side being thrown are the 5 chances that some other side will appear against the 1 chance that the specified side will be thrown. The odds, then, are 5 to 1 that the specified side will not appear. When the probability is $\frac{1}{36}$, the odds are 35 to 1. When the probability is $\frac{2}{36}$, the odds are 34 to 2, or 17 to 1.

If the gambling-house operator bets $35 to your $1 that a double ace (two aces) will not be thrown on the next roll of two dice, the betting odds are the same as the true or correct odds. In the long run he can expect to win at the rate of 35 out of every 36 bets, and you can expect to win at the rate of 1 out of every 36 bets. In the long run neither of you will win or lose, but will come out even, but it won't be a certainty. Professional gamblers call such a bet at true odds an even-up proposition. In general, odds may be defined as the advantage one bettor or competitor gives to another in proportion to the assumed risk, so that each has an equal chance. The gambling casino or gaming-house operator cannot afford to give players an even-up bet at any of his tables. As he says, "There's no percentage in that." He must, in some way, gain an advantage, or edge, over the player or players. He must have a better opportunity to win each bet than the player. He obtains it either by taking a direct charge or by paying off a player's winning bet at less than the correct odds—which results in a percentage profit for the gambling-house operator. However, in some games or bets the percentage, or P.C., is hidden in the subtle structure of the game itself, and is difficult to spot even by old-time gambling operators—the "Pass Line Bet" at Bank Craps proves the point. You place a $1 bet on the pass line; if you win, the dealer pays you $2 (your $1 plus the $1 you won). The house's edge of $1\frac{41}{99}$ percent is hidden in the mathematics and rules of the game, but it's there, silently working for the house. The operator's percentage is the price you pay for making use of the gambling facilities.

With few exceptions, the thousands of women whose gambling behavior I studied on my visits to racetracks, casinos, cardrooms, and bookie parlors made it a habit of placing all sorts of bets, and bucking various unknown high percentages, very often fighting such stiff odds that even when they hit a winning streak, and should have won, they ended as losers. Their chances to win were chopped down to almost nothing simply because they didn't know how to bet.

Most women gamblers today know—or should know—that the operator has a percentage edge in his favor; but because they can't or don't calculate, they never know how powerful it actually is; and because it usually works against them so smoothly and quietly they forget most of the time that it exists.

Here is a simple example that shows how percentage works and why it shouldn't be forgotten. Suppose you walk up to a Bank Craps table with 36 $1 bills and decide to make 36 consecutive bets of $1 each on the space of the table's layout marked "Two Aces." The house pays winners at odds of 30 to 1. We have previously learned that the correct odds of throwing two aces in one roll of the dice are 35 to 1, or that the chances of so doing are 1 in 36. You place a $1 bet on the "Two Aces" layout. Since the probability is $\frac{1}{36}$, you can expect in the long run to lose 35 bets for each one that you win.

Let's suppose that the dice act exactly this way in the first 36 throws of the dice—you lose the first 35 bets and you are out $35. You have only one buck left. Now you bet that. The two aces pop up, and you win. If the dealer paid off at the correct odds of 35 to 1, he would return the $1 you bet plus the $35 you won—you would break even with the $36 you had at the start.

But no gambling operator ever does this. In our example, since he pays off at 30 to 1 your win gets you $30. This with the $1 bet, which is returned to you, adds up to $31. You have $5 less than at the start. This $5 out of $36, or 13% percent, is the house's favorable percentage; it's his charge for operating the game.

Let's follow the above example further. Suppose you placed 360 consecutive $1 bets on the two aces, and for round figures let us assume Dame Fortune favored you a little above normal and you are averaging a loss of 10 cents (10 percent) instead of the expected 13% cents (13% percent) for each dollar that you bet. Your $36 bankroll will go up and down; but after you have made your 360th bet, you will on the average have lost 360 × 10 cents, or $36, and be broke. The above example, although in a different percentage ratio, holds true at the racetrack, Bingo parlor, Roulette, Baccarat, Blackjack, the slot machines, Keno, with the race and sports bookies, the Numbers game, and wheels of fortune.

By now you should understand how the operators' favorable percentages actually work and why operators of gambling schemes get rich and most players poor.

Millie, a woman crapshooter I interviewed at the Sands Hotel Casino in Las Vegas, is a typical example of how the majority of American Casino gamblers think. "Mr. Scarne," she said, "when I gamble here in Las Vegas, I follow the same system as I do when betting at the racetrack. If I think a horse is going to win, I bet him. I gamble the same way at the dice table. If I think a number is going to pop up, I bet it. It's about the same. If I pick the right horse or the right number, I win; if I don't, I lose."

I couldn't take exception to Millie's system of betting the horses for the obvious reason that the racetrack retains the same percentage on all bets. The track's percentage take at New York racetracks runs from 15 percent to 17 percent, and there is no legitimate way to reduce it no matter how you bet. But there are many ways to reduce the casino's percentage take at Bank Craps, Blackjack, Chemin de Fer, Roulette, and so on. In brief, the more you reduce the house percentages, the better are your chances of quitting the game a winner.

In the gambling casinos where I am a consultant, women often come up to me and say, "Mr. Scarne, can't you give me a system so I can beat this game?" They all get the same answer: "If there was any surefire legitimate system to beat these games, this casino would never have opened." There is nothing more futile than the attempt to evolve betting systems that will overcome adverse odds.

The oldest and commonest betting system is the martingale, or "doubling up," system, in which bets are doubled progressively. This probably dates back to the Stone Age, but every day of the week some woman or male gambler somewhere reinvents it, or some variation of it, and believes she has something new. Over the years hundreds of "surefire" winning systems have been dreamed up, and not one of them is worth the price of yesterday's newspaper.

The reason is simple. When you make a bet at less than the correct odds, which you always do in any organized gambling operation, you are paying the operator a direct charge or a percentage charge for the privilege of making the bet. Your chance of winning has what mathematicians call a "minus expectation." When you use a system you make a series of bets, each of which has a minus expectation. There is no way of adding minuses to get a plus, or of adding losses to show a profit.

Add to this the fact that all gambling operators, including

race and sports bookies, limit the size of the player's wagers so that it is impossible to double up bets indefinitely. This and the house percentage make all gambling systems worthless.

The sole exception is in games of both chance and skill (Poker, Gin Rummy, Bridge, Cribbage, Private Craps, and so on) when the player has some special skill or knowledge that enables her to make most of her bets with a plus expectation. As an example, suppose a certain bridge team is a 2 to 1 favorite to win your local tournament because the state's top-ranking player is captain of that team. If you obtain inside information that he has suffered an illness that will keep him out of the tournament, and if you then get 2 to 1 odds on the second-choice team, you would have a plus expectation.

The system player believes her system will overcome the operator's favorable edge. She couldn't be more wrong. Systems actually work against the player and for the operator because they are all based on a combination or series of bets, and the more bets the system player makes, the more she increases the operator's percentage take.

Gambling operators as a rule love system players because they have to bet a specified amount of money, usually more than the average player bets, in order to back up the system. The system demands that the player bet it all, and the gambling operator knows he is going to get it all.

If a woman gambler with $100 wants merely to double it, the soundest plan is to risk it all in one bet that pays off at even money and possesses a low house percentage. When she splits her $100 into smaller bets, as she would have to do in playing most systems, she merely reduces her chance of doubling her money; the smaller the bets, the less chance she has.

What causes women to believe in gambling systems? Women, more so than men, seem to fall for the stories they have heard or read about some scientific gambler or mathematics professor who has spent years doping out a surefire gambling system, which he later used to break the bank at Monte Carlo or Las Vegas.

The years 1962 to 1965 were banner years for stories of this kind. During these years considerable publicity appeared in the American press concerning Edward O. Thorp, a New Mexico State University mathematics professor, a man who claimed that he had devised a surefire legitimate system of beating the Blackjack tables in Las Vegas. Perhaps you saw one of the many feature stories about Thorp and his Blackjack system that appeared in various national periodicals, including *Life, Reader's Digest, Sports Illustrated, Time, Newsweek,* and others. The *Life* article described Thorp as "The Greatest System Player of All Time," a man who, if given the opportunity to play his system, was sure to win some $300,000 a month bucking the Blackjack dealer.

On April 28, 1964, I challenged Professor Thorp and his millionaire backers, Mr. X and Mr. Y, to a $100,000 Blackjack Contest at the Sands Hotel Casino in Las Vegas, Nevada, a match that would test the worth of Thorp's Blackjack system. Thorp's reply to my $100,000 Blackjack challenge was a *big No.*

Early in 1965, another mathematician, by the name of Dr. Allan N. Wilson, broke into book print by stating that he had a so-called infallible Blackjack system much better than Thorp's because with the Wilson system even an amateur player was guaranteed to get rich at the casino tables. What hokum!

Professor Edward O. Thorp and Dr. Allan N. Wilson claim that their Blackjack systems are infallible. However, if you ask each why he doesn't take his infallible system to Nevada, Puerto Rico, or the Grand Bahamas and win all the money he and his family will ever need, he will probably tell you that casino operators know about him and his infallible system and won't let him gamble. Casinos in Puerto Rico are run under government supervision, and no legitimate gambler can be barred from playing in Puerto Rican casinos. So come on down, boys, and get rich. Last year several women followers of Dr. Wilson's system came to Puerto Rico, lost their bankroll, and had to borrow money to return home.

What does Dr. Wilson actually think of his infallible Blackjack system? Not much when it comes to putting money on the line. This was proved by a law student named Kenneth Hense, who challenged Dr. Allan N. Wilson to a $5,000 head-to-head Blackjack contest, and Dr. Wilson refused his challenge. Later I received the silent treatment to a $100,000 B.J. challenge I flung at Dr. Allan Wilson. This challenge was issued in my autobiography *The Odds Against Me*.

Owing to the fact that thousands of unsuspecting women gamblers fall for these so-called surefire winning systems, with which they lose their hard-earned cash, it is my duty as a gambling expert to expose every one of these ridiculous get-rich-quick gambling schemes.

As further proof of the futility of all legitimate gambling systems, let me tell you the story of the most talked-about system player who ever gambled at Monte Carlo, the world's most famous casino. It all began on a July day in 1891 when an English thief and con man, Charles Wells, sat down to play Roulette with a £4,000 bankroll of swindled money. He faced exposure and imprisonment if he lost; but after eleven hours of play he had won 250,000 francs (about $50,000). Two days later he broke the bank a dozen times. This is not so profitable as it sounds, because it was not the casino bank, but merely the 100,000-franc bank at the Roulette table. Wells claimed his success was due to an infallible system, and he became famous overnight. His phenomenal luck persisted, and at the season's end he returned to England a winner, although grossly exaggerating the profits, which he soon spent. His fame and his ability as a con man enabled him to acquire another bankroll from backers who swallowed his system story, and he returned to Monte Carlo in 1892. Again he broke the bank on this occasion, six times, before his luck deserted him and he lost everything. On his way back to England, he was arrested on charges of fraud, was tried in Old Bailey, and sentenced to an eight-year prison term. Later swindles got him another three-year stretch in England, and one of five years in France.

Even if the casino had never regained in 1892 any of the money Wells had won the season before, the operators would still have profited enormously, because Charles Wells became the hero of an international song hit that advertised the casino throughout the world: "The Man Who Broke the Bank at Monte Carlo." Shortly before his death, in 1922, he admitted that he had played strictly according to a system only during the second season, when he had lost.

In this book I analyze the mistakes that most women gamblers make most often and find most costly. Usually a gambler can easily avoid such mistakes if she knows the few basic and generally simple principles that govern her favorite gambling game. Pay attention to these principles, and you are certain to improve your chances of going home a winner.

The best way to improve your chance of winning is first to learn the rules of your favorite gambling pastime, and then to have a good working knowledge of the adverse odds and percentages in that game. In the following pages you will find all this information, and more, concerning the most popular women's gambling activities and games played here and abroad.

3

Bank Craps

Women seldom indulged in crapshooting until about twenty years ago. The game was considered undignified before it appeared in swank gambling establishments in the form of Bank Craps—an invention of an old-time friend of mine, John H. Winn. My survey shows that today approximately 3 million women play Craps in one form or another.

If you took time out to clock the number of women shooting Craps in the plush casinos on the Las Vegas Strip for a full evening, your clocking would show that about 1 out of every 10 crapshooters is a woman. You'd get the same clocking results in the plush casinos in the Caribbean islands, at Monte Carlo, and wherever legally operated crap games are found.

One reason for the popularity of Craps is that Craps offers the players a greater chance of participation than any other casino game. In Roulette, the croupier spins the wheel, and at Blackjack the dealer turns up the cards, and so it goes with other casino games. But in Bank Craps, when the woman picks up the dice she feels that she has control of her destiny. The thrill she gets when she matches her luck against that of the house is of a more personal kind than the one she gets when she simply waits and hopes that the little ivory ball will drop into her number or that the stone-faced Blackjack dealer will hit her with the desired card.

Bank Craps' popularity with women is also due to its two-way action. In most casino games the player can bet only that a certain event will happen. She can't bet it won't; the house does that. But in most Bank Craps games, the player may bet either "do or don't." She can bet with the shooter or against the shooter, as she likes. But in only one sense is this statement true. Actually, you're not betting with or against the shooter—you're betting against the house either way you look at it. If you win, the house pays you. If you lose, the house takes your money. This, plus the fact that many different types of bets can be placed on the table's layout, gives Bank Craps an unequaled rapidity of action and a thrill and excitement no other casino game has ever offered. The real lady gambler is impatient, and when she has once tasted the fast action of Craps, other casino games seem dull and slow.

Speaking of lady crapshooters, do you know that the world's crapshooting record for consecutive passes is held by a woman? It took place on the evening of January 18, 1952, at the Caribe Hilton Hotel Casino, in San Juan, Puerto Rico. It all started that evening at exactly 9:00 P.M., one hour after the casino doors were first opened to the public. I was standing in the dice pit, watching the action at one of the casino's dice tables. The dice were acting in favor of the house: a pass (the shooter wins), a missout (the shooter loses), another pass, another missout. That was exactly how the dice were behaving that evening until the stickman pushed the pair of dice in front of a woman and said, "Lady, you're the next shooter."

She shook her head, and replied, "I don't like throwing the dice—I just like to bet with the shooter."

A man next to her, who I later learned was her husband, nudged her and said: "Ethel, go ahead; shoot the dice. I think you're lucky tonight."

Ethel flashed him a smile and said, "I don't like to shoot the dice"; then she hesitated a moment, and continued, "All right, honey, just this one time."

Ethel placed a $1 chip on the line (the indicated space on the table where you place your bet that the shooter will win), picked up the dice, and, without bothering to shake them, employed an overhand throwing movement, letting the dice fly across the surface of the table. They came to a stop near the center.

"Seven, the winner. Pay the line," cried the stickman. This was the beginning of an incredible dice roll that was to make gambling history. Ethel continued making pass after pass. After each pass she removed her $1 winnings from the Pass Line.

After throwing ten successive passes, her husband cried out: "Honey, double up your bet. You're on a lucky streak."

"Every time I increase my bet I'm sure to miss my point number," she replied matter of factly.

"Okay, honey, do as you wish," answered her husband.

Ethel held on to the dice for approximately 90 minutes. In that 90-minute period I saw a new world's record made at the Craps table—39 straight passes.

Despite this fantastic accomplishment, Ethel won only $38. Not knowing how to bet her money, she continued to place her lone $1 chip on the line. The male "do (win) bettors" cleaned up a bundle on Ethel's hot roll—one, in particular, won $7,500 with an original $20 bankroll. All the male "don't (shooter will lose) bettors" were taken to the cleaners. At the end of the evening the dice table showed a loss of $35,000—quite a sum when we consider that the maximum limit for a single bet at the Caribe Hilton Casino dice tables is only $100.

Ethel's husband, who knew just a little more than she about Bank Craps, won several hundred dollars.

Ethel's manner of shooting Craps is a classic example of what I would call the worst kind of gambling possible. She, like most women, not having the least knowledge of how to bet her money, passed up a golden opportunity that should have netted her at least several thousand dollars instead of a mere $38.

Later, I calculated Ethel's feat of making 39 straight passes to be about 1 in 956 billion—to be exact: 1 in 956,211,843,725.

But don't think for a moment that all women gamblers are as meek as Ethel—not by a long shot.

The fair sex has its quota of shrewd high-rolling dice players. The most notable one I ever met was a seventy-two-year-old widow known to Nevada casino operators as "Ma." I saw her last one day in Las Vegas, when she entered Joe Brown's downtown Horseshoe Club and asked Joe if he would ante up his maximum $300 Craps limit for her.

"Ma," Joe said, "you can have any betting limit you want, but your maximum will be determined by the amount of your first bet."

Ma didn't bat an eye. "I understand, Mr. Brown. My first wager is $10,000 on the Pass Line."

She took her place at the table, began putting ten-grand bets on the Craps layout, and within thirty minutes had won a cool $70,000. That evening, after Ma had departed with her winnings, Joe Brown called me aside and said: "Scarne, I must have been off my rocker to give that old lady a $10,000 limit. From now on, she'll have to be satisfied with my $300 limit or take her business down the street. In the past six weeks that old lady has taken me and a couple of other Las Vegas casino owners for some $250,000 by getting us to increase our betting limit at the Craps table."

About a year later, after having lost more than $2 million at the $300 maximum-limit dice tables, she disappeared from the Nevada casinos. Joe Brown later told me that she was the fastest woman Craps player he had ever seen and that as a big-time bettor she held her own with the few outstanding male high rollers.

The fault of most present-day women dice players is that they get carried away with the excitement generated by a fast-action Craps game, and make all sorts of bets they shouldn't make. Many of them are under the impression that every high roller they see gambling at the dice table is a sharp, shrewd

Craps player. This belief causes them to lose money by making the same kind of bets. The truth of the matter is that most male big bettors are in the same boat as she is. They may even know less than she does about the house odds they are out to beat.

Many women dice players that I scouted over the years cultivated the friendship of casino dealers in the hope that the advice they received would help them to beat the game. I agree wholeheartedly with Major Riddle, boss of the Las Vegas Dunes Casino, when he says: "These men, for the most part, are losers over a period of time. They think they know how to gamble, but their bankbooks and the fact that they are working for a wage prove that they really know very little about the actual mathematics of the game they deal." I agree. I've watched hundreds of casino employees gamble over the years. Most of them, like the majority of players they deal to, are real suckers at gambling. They make it a habit to bet on hunches, omens, and superstitions instead of the house percentages.

Many women casino gamblers I've talked to shy away from the Craps table because the fast action and wide variety of different type of bets made at dice tables appear to them very confusing and complicated. The truth is that Craps is an easier game to play than Blackjack, Chemin de Fer, or Baccarat, favored by the same women.

Let's move over to the dice table and see what is taking place. Bets are down, and one of the players is about to toss the two dice onto the table. She's called the "shooter," and the first roll of the dice is called a "come-out."

Let's say that the shooter has made a bet that she'll pass or win. The shooter wins immediately if on the come-out she rolls a 7 or 11, and loses immediately if on the come-out she rolls a 2, 3, or 12. The 7 and 11 are called "naturals"; 2, 3, and 12 are called "craps."

On the other hand, if on the come-out she doesn't roll a natural or a crap, and instead rolls either 4, 5, 6, 8, 9, or 10— whichever of these she rolls now becomes her "point" and she continues rolling until she either wins by rolling her point once again or loses by rolling a 7. Notice that 7 works two ways; it wins for the shooter on the come-out, and it loses for her anytime she makes it while trying for her point number.

The shooter retains the dice as long as she continues to roll naturals and craps and make-points. When she rolls a 7 while trying for a point, she loses the dice, and the shooter to her left becomes the next shooter, who may decline to shoot the dice; and the person to her left becomes the next shooter, and so on.

That's the story of Bank Craps from the shooter's point of view. However, before you can consider yourself a Bank Craps player, you must know the different wagers and pay-off odds that may be made at the dice table.

And so let's take a look at the dice table itself.

The table is about the size of a standard pool or billiard table, with a 10-inch upright wooden rail running around the table's outside edges—forming a rectangular enclosure. The rail serves as a backboard, and also helps to prevent the rolling dice from falling off the table.

Modern dice tables have grooves running around the top edges of the rail. The grooves are for the players to place their chips so that they do not clutter up the table's playing surface. The inside of the four-sided rail is lined with sponge rubber embossed in various patterns to ensure that the dice rebound in a random manner. Gambling-house operators, well aware that there are nimble-fingered players who have spent years mastering the art of making honest dice roll in a predetermined manner, insist that any shooter suspected of trying to control by sliding one or both dice across the center of the table must throw the cubes so that they strike the rubber-covered backboard and bounce back at random before coming to a stop.

A full working dice table on the Las Vegas Strip requires a minimum of four men to operate. Harold's Club, Reno's number-one gambling casino, employs only women dealers at its gaming tables. For speed and efficiency in dealing at Craps, several of the girl dealers I scouted at Harold's Club during my survey put many a Las Vegas male dice dealer to shame.

The four men required to run a dice table include three

dealers and a boxman. The boxman is the man who sits at the table's center—he is the boss. His duty is to keep his eyes on everything—dice, money, chips, players, dealers, and so on. Two of the dealers stand on each side of him. After each dice decision, the dealers rake in the losses and pay off the winnings. The third dealer, who stands opposite the boxman, has charge of the dice. He is often referred to as the "stickman" because he retrieves the dice after each roll with a curved stick and holds them until such time as all previous bets have been settled and new bets made. Whereupon, with the stick he pushes the dice toward the shooter.

The table's surface is covered with a tight-fitting green baize cloth on which are printed two exact large-sized designs separated at the table's center by another large design allocated for various side bets. The purpose of the duplicate designs is to accommodate more players and to permit them to make their bets without leaning forward too far or leaving their places at the table. Because of these duplicate layout designs, the Craps table itself is called a double side dealer. Each of these designs is divided into spaces, of different shapes and sizes, representing the various bets that can be placed against the house. This green baize table covering is known as a "Craps layout." Although there are numerous differently shaped layouts, the actual difference is small. Some layouts carry one or two wagers that others don't have; some differ more or less in the odds offered. This last variation depends directly upon the players who patronize that particular casino—how much they know about dice odds and how much of a house percentage they will stand to buck. The smarter the patronage, the better the odds approach the correct ones; the less they know, the greater the house percentages.

All Craps layouts are clever exercises in mathematics designed to give the player an exciting run for her money—and at the same time give the house a mathematical edge on every bet shown on the layout.

The majority of women crap players know little or nothing about the house percentages they are fighting, and this lack of knowledge puts them in the chump, or sucker, category. The following odds and percentages will tell you how to stop being a chump and become as gambling wise as the most seasoned male dice gambler found in Las Vegas or anywhere else.

Before we begin our analysis of Bank Craps odds and percentages, you must remember that if you become a habitual crapshooter, you will lose no matter how smart you bet. It makes no difference in the long run whether you make bets having less than 1 percent against you or whether you place bets that have a big 16⅔ percent going against you. Over a long period of play, the house's percentage is bound to take both the smart dice player and the chump. The only difference is that the chump doesn't even have a fighting chance—she *gives* her money to the house.

I promised to tell you how to bet and how to become as gambling wise as the top male professional gamblers in Las Vegas. All the necessary information required to achieve this aim is contained in the following pages. The rest is up to you. So, if you want to bet as do the smartest male gamblers of Las Vegas, give the following text some serious study. Now, first let's analyze the bets that these shrewd high-rolling male gamblers of Las Vegas make at Bank Craps, starting with the line bets.

Line Bets: There are two different types of line bets—the Pass Line bet and the Don't Pass Line bet. Each bet can be made only before a come-out roll. After the come-out, they cannot be withdrawn. First to be discussed is the Pass Line.

Pass Line—also referred to on different layouts as "Pass," "Line," "Win," or "Do": The lady who wants to bet the house that the shooter will win, that the dice will pass, places her chip or chips, before the come-out, on the long narrow space of the layout printed with any of the following words: Pass Line, Pass, Line, Win, or Do.

This bet is without a doubt the most popular bet made by male players at the Craps table because it's the bet they first learned when shooting Craps in some vacant lot or back room.

The house pays this bet off at even money (1 to 1), and enjoys a favorable edge of 1.414 percent, or about 7 cents on a $5 wager. Owing to the house's low percentage take, this is one of the wisest casino bets a player can make. But most women players are attracted by other bets that pay off at bigger odds; and because they don't know odds, they don't know they are fighting greater house percentages.

Like all bets placed on the Craps layout, this wager can be made by any player, whether he is the shooter or not; however, it cannot be withdrawn—it remains until it's won or lost.

Don't Pass Line—also referred to on different layouts as either "Don't" or "Lose": The lady who wants to bet that the shooter will lose, that the dice will not pass, places her chip or chips, before the come-out, on the small corner layout space marked Don't Pass, Don't, or Lose. The house pays off at even money (1 to 1). If you were to make this bet in a private or noncommercial crap game, you'd have an advantage, for, as I told you above, the shooter has a 1.414 percent disadvantage.

Remember this, however: you are not playing in a private crap game—you're playing in a gambling casino—and casinos wouldn't stay in business long if they took a beating of 1.414 percent. The casino resorts, therefore, to a simple tactical maneuver: it bars the two 6's (or the two 1's) on the come-out roll. This means that if on the come-out the shooter makes a 12 or a 2 (crap), your bet is a standoff; there is no action for the player or players who have placed bets on the spaces of the layout marked, Don't Pass, Don't, or Lose. In a private or non-commercial game of Craps the fader or wrong bettor would have won the bet, but at the Bank Craps table it is no decision for the Don't bettor.

By barring the two 6's or two 1's in this bet, the house is taking away the 1.414 percent edge you would have had, and has replaced it with a house advantage of 1.402 percent or about 7 cents on a $5 wager.

So for all practical reasons it doesn't matter whether you bet the Pass Line or Don't Pass Line; the house percentage remains about the same.

However, because this wager has a standoff, women players

think erroneously that it has a much higher house percentage than it actually does—hence you'll seldom find women betting the Don't Pass Line.

If the house bars the two 1's (aces) instead of two 6's, as some do, it gets the same results as if it were barring two 6's. When some houses bar the 3 (ace and deuce or 1 and 2) instead of the double 6 or double 1 (ace), the 4.385 percent in its favor has not merely doubled—as so many women players think—it has more than tripled! And when you see a layout that bars the 3, forget it exists.

Come and Don't Come: The lady who wishes to bet on the Come or Don't Come places her bet on the spaces of the layout marked Come or Don't Come. These bets were put there to help speed up the line action; because even if a shooter is trying for a point number, a bettor can put her money on the layout and bet as she would on the come-out.

The Come bet is essentially the same as the Pass Line bet, and the Don't Come mimics the Don't Pass bet, except that the Come and Don't Come bets are made after the come-out. Both are paid off at even money, and the house percentages on these wagers are the same as on the Pass Line and Don't Pass Line bets, which is 1.414 percent, or about 7 cents on a $5 wager, made on the Come, and 1.402 percent, or about 7 cents on a $5 wager, made on the Don't Come.

Suppose you put a chip on the space of the layout marked Come, the first roll of the dice is the point number as far as you're concerned. For example, the shooter is trying to make her point, which happens to be 8. You make a bet on the Come, and on the next roll the shooter throws a 5, your point number is 5. In every subsequent roll of the dice, your Come bet stands until either a 5 is made and you win, or a 7 is made and you lose. This also holds true for the Don't Come bet in relation to a Don't Pass bet—even to the bar on the two 6's. Come or Don't Come bets, like line bets, cannot be withdrawn; they remain until they are won or lost.

Free Odds Bets: Here is how the smart woman "Do bettor" can slice down the house's edge of 1.414 percent on the Pass

Line and Come bets to less than 1 percent by taking the odds that the shooter will make her point number. When you have made a Pass Line or Come bet, and the shooter already has come-out on a point or new number, you're allowed to make a free second bet, limited to the amount of your wager on the Pass Line or Come, that the shooter will make her point number. This is called "taking the odds," which means that the house will give you the true odds that the shooter won't make the point. The true or correct odds on each point number are as follows:

Odds Against Making the Point Numbers

The Point Numbers	Correct Odds	Correct Payoff Odds in Dollars
4 or 10	2 to 1	$2.00 to $1.00
5 or 9	3 to 2	$1.50 to $1.00
6 or 8	6 to 5	$1.20 to $1.00

Let's say that you have a $10 bet riding on the Pass Line, and on the come-out the shooter rolls a 4; the above chart reveals that the correct odds against the shooter making this point are 2 to 1. If you want to "take the odds," you place an additional $10 on the layout directly behind your $10 Pass Line wager. If the shooter makes the 4, the house pays you $20 for the second bet plus $10 for your original Pass Line bet.

When you have a bet riding on the Pass Line, it's always advantageous to take the free odds on the point, since this reduces the 1.414 percent the house originally had on the Pass Line bet to less than 1 percent—to be exact .848 of 1 percent.

However, if you're one of the few women who do bet the Don't Pass Line, remember that the house will allow you to "lay the odds" on the point equal to your Don't Pass Line or Don't Come bet. Suppose the point is 4 again, and you have $10 riding on the Don't Pass Line and you want to lay the odds that the shooter will not make it; you put down any even amount up to $20. When you *take* the odds on a Pass bet, you are limited to the amount of your line bet. But when you lay the odds on a Don't Pass bet, you are limited to the amount that could give you winnings of not higher than your original bet. If the shooter fails to make the point, the house pays you $10 for each of your two winning bets. The house advantage on both these wagers also runs to less than 1 percent—to be exact .832 of 1 percent.

The Free Odds bets made on the Pass Line, Don't Pass Line, Come or Don't Come may be taken down (removed) at any time before the bet is decided.

One thing should be remembered, however: The lowest-valued chip in a luxury casino is a $1 chip, and for that reason dealers cannot pay off on any part of a dollar. Therefore, when you're taking the free odds make sure that your bet doesn't pay off in cents. For example, if your Pass Line bet was $1, the point was 5; taking the free odds for $1 would hurt you rather than benefit you simply because the dice dealer would not pay you the $1.50 your bet should bring. You would be paid one lone $1 chip—that's all. To bet the correct odds of 3 to 2, your Pass Line bet should have been $2.

The only way to take *full* advantage of the free odds is to make your bet a minimum (or multiple) of ten ($10). Since the average woman Pass Line bettor usually bets only a buck or two, she cannot take full advantage of the free odds. Here's why: When you make your Pass Line bet, you don't know what the come-out number will be. If you bet $1, and the come-out is 4 or 10, you're all right. You can get the full 2-to-1 odds. If the come-out is 5, 6, or 9, you can't. You'd get $1 to $1 instead of $1.50 to $1 on the 5 or 9. You'd get even money instead of 6–5 on the 6 or 8. Similarly, every bet up to $10, you'd be blocked from getting full odds on one or another number. But on a $10 bet, you can get 2–1, 3–2, or 6–5, depending on the come-out number. This is true of any multiple of 10, but not of any other number or multiple. You can figure it yourself. This does not mean that you have to bet $10. With a smaller bet you can still find free odds on some numbers, though not all.

If you happen to be in a situation like that described above, and the Craps dealer tries to induce you to increase the amount of your Pass Line bet after the come-out by telling you that it is to your best advantage since it will permit you to take full advantage of the free-odds' offer, *don't*. Acceptance is to take even money instead of odds that the shooter will make her point, and the Free Odds bet is no longer free.

Although "betting the line" and taking or laying the free odds as described above is the smartest way of gambling at casino dice tables—it is strange how very, very few women gamblers take full advantage of such a play. I have found that many women are just as unpredictable as the dice. During the thrill, action, and excitement of the game, they bet as their emotions, rather than their minds, dictate. They follow their intuition rather than their knowledge of the game, and seldom do the right thing at the right time.

Place Bets: Now we come to two spaces of the layout exactly similar in design, and with each situated nearest the dealer. Each design depicts six large boxed numbers that read 4, 5, 6, 8, 9, 10. These are called "Place Numbers," and are similar to the Free Odds bets discussed above, such as taking or laying the odds that the shooter will or will not throw a given number or numbers before making a 7. Most women gamblers don't bet the place numbers until after a come-out. However, place bets can be made at any time, and withdrawn whenever desired.

The two major differences between a Free Odds bet and a Place Number bet is that when you bet a place number you don't have to make a line bet first; and, unlike the Free Odds bet, you may bet one or all six place numbers at any time before the next roll of the dice. But for this privilege the house charges you a percentage fee for each and every place bet you make.

This is usually 5 percent, and you have to give the dealer that 5 percent in chips or cash. In some cases the house extracts its percentage by paying off place bets at less than the correct odds, instead of charging a fee. The following chart gives the house payoff odds, correct odds, and the favorable house advantage in terms of percentage and money, on all the possible place bets that can be made at Bank Craps:

Bank's Favorable Percentages on Place Bets			
House's Payoff Odds	Correct Odds	Percentage in House's Favor	House Percentage on $5 bet
House lays 9 to 5 on 4 or 10	10 to 5	6.666%	About 33 cents
House lays 7 to 5 on 5 or 9	7½ to 5	4.000%	About 20 cents
House lays 7 to 6 on 6 or 8	6 to 5	1.515%	About 8 cents
Player lays 11 to 5 on 4 or 10	10 to 5	3.030%	About 15 cents
Player lays 8 to 5 on 5 or 9	7½ to 5	2.500%	About 12 cents
Player lays 5 to 4 on 6 or 8	6 to 5	1.818%	About 9 cents

Obviously the best place bet is to take the 7 to 6 odds on the 6 or 8, since the house's favorable advantage is 1.515 percent, or about 8 cents on a $5 bet. However, most women players, as you'll learn later, insist on putting their money on the big 6 or big 8, which returns only even money, thus costing 9 1/11 percent, or about 46 cents on the same wager. This is a perfect example of foolish betting at the dice table.

Most luxury casinos on the Las Vegas Strip, including the

Sands, Dunes, Desert Inn, Flamingo, and Caesars Palace, in addition to permitting place bets, also allow players to "buy the numbers." In buying the numbers, the player is paid off at correct odds, such as 6 to 5 on 6 or 8, 3 to 2 on 5 or 9, and 2 to 1 on 4 or 10. However, for such services, the bank levies a direct charge of 5 percent payable in advance on the total sum wagered; this amounts to a charge of $1 on each $20 bet, which happens to be the minimum bet permitted at Strip casinos where bets of this type are allowed.

Buying the numbers is favored by male gamblers hailing from New York, New Jersey, and other eastern states, and is not recommended for women.

A number of casinos in this country and the Caribbean islands operate their Bank Craps tables by compelling players to buy the numbers. Place, Come and Don't Come free Back-Line bets are not permitted. The most notable casino of this kind is the plush El Casino in Freeport, Grand Bahamas. This type of game is known as New York Craps. There is one very peculiar fact about the direct 5 percent charge: in most games, the house's favorable percentage is greater than most women players think, but the 5 percent charge at New York Craps is less than nearly all crap players and most casino operators suspect. Here are the correct percentages in favor of the house when the operators levy a 5 percent charge:

The Do Bettor pays $1, or 4.761 percent, when taking $20 worth of odds on the numbers 4, 5, 6, 8, 9, or 10.

The Don't Bettor pays $1, or 2.439 percent, when laying odds of $40 to $20 on the numbers 4 or 10.

The Don't Bettor pays $1, or 3.225 percent, when laying odds of $30 to $20 on the numbers 5 or 9.

The Don't Bettor pays $1, or 4 percent, when laying odds of $24 to $20 on the numbers 6 or 8.

In Bank Craps games that permit a player to make a place bet *or* buy the numbers at 5 percent, it would be to a player's advantage to buy the 4 and 10 and place the 5, 9, 6, and 8.

It soon becomes clear that once you've learned the basic rules of Bank Craps, the bets that may be made on the Craps layout aren't at all difficult to understand. The trouble with the average woman player lies not in not knowing how to play the game, but in knowing little or nothing about odds and house percentages she is out to beat. As a result, in a game where she has an opportunity to slice the house edge down to less than 1 percent, as explained in the foregoing, she insists on making all sorts of ridiculous side bets where at times she's bucking a house edge as high as 16⅔ percent. Side bets are called "propositional bets" by casino operators. I call them by their right name: "sucker bets."

Let's analyze some of these ridiculous bets favored by most women dice players, starting with Field bets.

Field Bets: Most of the women crap players whom I have observed playing Bank Craps are suckers for Field bets. The crap stickman, at the sight of a woman player, begins to sell the Field bets by chanting constantly during the game: "Place your bet on the field. Nine, that's a field number. Ten, another field number." When she hesitates, he adds obligingly that the field has seven winning numbers and only four losing numbers. After this pitch, she usually begins betting the field.

The field usually bears the numbers, 2, 3, 5, 9, 10, 11, and 12. When the player puts her bet on the space of the layout marked "Field" she is betting that one of the group of seven numbers listed there will be thrown on the next roll. The bank pays even money. Since the field shows seven numbers, and there are only four (4, 6, 7, and 8) that can make her lose, the nonthinker figures that her chances are excellent. She may even believe that she has the best of it or, at the very least, an even chance. But appearances are nearly always deceptive, especially in casino games.

If we add together all the ways in which the winning and losing numbers can be thrown, we find that the above field numbers can be made in only 17 ways as against 19 ways for the losing numbers. The house, consequently, has an advantage of 5⅝ percent, or about 28 cents on a $5 bet.

Other layouts are made with the 4 in place of the 5, so that the field bears the numbers 2, 3, 4, 9, 10, 11, and 12, and pay double on 1 and 12; others pay 3 to 1 on 2. In each case the player's disadvantage is still $5\frac{5}{9}$ percent or about 28 cents on a $5 bet.

The lure of Craps is its fast action, but because wagers on the field are either won or lost every time the dice are rolled, the action is so fast and furious that most women's bankrolls can't take it. With the $5\frac{5}{9}$ percent grinding away and taking $\frac{1}{18}$ of every bet you make, the house can expect to eat up the amount of your wager in 18 rolls.

To show what this means in dollars and cents, let us assume that you place 180 Field bets of $10 each, which you can do in an hour's time at many fast-action crap tables, and assume that the law of averages works according to expectation. This hour of field betting would cost you exactly $100.

It's a cinch that the lady field bettor who believes that her chances of winning are excellent has not looked at the following chart, which shows all the 36 possible combinations that can be made with 2 dice:

36 Combinations or Ways with 2 Dice

2 can be made in 1 way:	1–1				
3 can be made in 2 ways:	1–2	2–1			
4 can be made in 3 ways:	1–3	3–1	2–2		
5 can be made in 4 ways:	1–4	4–1	2–3	3–2	
6 can be made in 5 ways:	1–5	5–1	2–4	4–2	3–3
7 can be made in 6 ways:	1–6	6–1	2–5	5–2	3–4	4–3
8 can be made in 5 ways:	2–6	6–2	3–5	5–3	4–4
9 can be made in 4 ways:	3–6	6–3	4–5	5–4	
10 can be made in 3 ways:	4–6	6–4	5–5		
11 can be made in 2 ways:	5–6	6–5			
12 can be made in 1 way:	6–6				

When we know that there are 36 ways of making the 11 numbers, and also how many ways each number can be made, we can easily obtain the true odds and house percentages on most bets made at Bank Craps. The general rule for figuring dice percentages is simply this: The house's favorable percentage is the number of ways the player is short divided by the total number of ways the event can happen. In the field above, the house has 19 ways to the player's 17. The player is short 2 ways. Divide 2 by 36 (total number of ways), and you get 5⅚ percent in favor of the house.

Next we come to what I consider one of the most foolish side bets found on the layout.

The Big 6 and the Big 8: The lady who places her bet on the spaces of the layout marked "big 6" or "big 8" is wagering that the number will be thrown before a 7. She can put her money on that space at any time. The bank pays even money, and most players labor under the impression that it is an even-money bet. The 6 and 8 spaces on most layouts are usually made large and are positioned where the players can reach them easily. Why any woman should think the bank would emphasize a bet that gives the house no percentage at all is a mystery.

A woman dice player at Bud Sweet's Bonaire Casino in the Netherland Antilles, once offered to bet me the 6's and 8's are thrown just as often as 7's. What the woman persisted in overlooking was that the male smart-money players who never bet the big 6 or the big 8 would, if her theory were correct, concentrate entirely on those bets. Eventually other players would follow suit; and in the long run, instead of showing a profit, the house would merely break even on the betting, and have nothing in the cashbox with which to pay operating, maintenance, and other costs. Since the casino is a business proposition, and the operator is not running it for the thrill of gambling, this just doesn't make sense. The very fact that the 6 and 8 spaces are made large and/or convenient to entice bets should be sufficient proof that the 6 and 8 can't possibly be even-money bets.

We know from our Combinations and Ways table that since either 6 or 8 can be made five ways and 7 in six ways, the correct odds are 6 to 5, or $1.20 to $1.00. The house's advantage is 9¹¹⁄₁₁ percent, which amounts to about 45 cents on a $5 bet.

The 6 and 8 spaces on most layouts have grown large and have come to be known as the big 6 and big 8 not because they are the best bet on the layout, but because the house has such a big edge. They are strictly sucker bets.

Smart-money male gamblers wouldn't touch such a bet with a ten-foot pole—especially when they know they can *place* the 6 and 8 and get far better odds.

Again, why most women gamblers insist on putting their money on the big 6 or big 8, and pay a whopping house percentage of 9¹¹⁄₁₁ percent, or 46 cents on a $5 bet, when they can just as easily *place* the 6 or 8 and pay a low house percentage of 1.515 percent, or about 8 cents on a $5 bet, is to me a perfect example of foolish betting by women crapshooters.

Hard-Way Bets: Another ridiculous type of side bet is to wager on one of four spaces in the center of the layout headed by the words "hard way." This is to bet that the shooter will make a specified even number (4, 6, 8, or 10) with two double numbers (hard way) before it is made the "easy way" (any way other than a hard way), or before a 7 is made. Hard-Way bets can be made at any time and withdrawn at any time.

Hard-Way wagers can be found on all layouts; and, once again, most women believe that the odds offered by the bank are fair enough. Some women even think they are getting correct odds, a lack of logic that almost classes as not thinking at all!

The layout not only does not offer correct odds on any of these bets; in many cases it offers even less than it appears to. This misdirection, as gamblers call it, is accomplished by wording the Craps layout so as to mislead players who forget that the two little words "for" and "to" do not mean the same thing. You will see how this deception operates in the following analysis of the Hard-Way wagers:

4 (2 and 2) and 10 (5 and 5) pay 7 to 1; the hard-way 6 (3 and 3) and the hard-way 8 (4 and 4) pays 9 to 1. The correct odds are 8 to 1 and 10 to 1, so that the house has a $9\frac{1}{11}$ percent, or about a 45-cent edge, against the woman who bets on the hard-way 6 and 8; and a $11\frac{1}{9}$ percent, or about a 56-cent edge, against her when she bets on the hard-way 4 or 10.

Some of the smaller casinos pay only 6 to 1 on the hard 4 and hard 10, and 8 to 1 on the hard 6 and hard 8—only, it doesn't look that way. The following example shows how this misdirection is achieved—the Craps layout is made to read 7 for 1 above the hard 4 and hard 10, and 9 for 1 above the hard 6 and hard 8. The difference is this: When paying off a $1 bet at 7-to-1 odds, the house gives you $7 and the $1 you bet; when paying off at 7-for-1 odds, the house keeps the $1 you bet. Some of the larger casinos make use of this same gimmick to mislead players in believing they are getting larger odds by having their layout read 8 for 1 on the hard 4 and the hard 10, and 10 for 1 on the hard 6 and hard 8.

Most women dice players with whom I've discussed the Hard-Way bets find it difficult to understand why the player gets 9 to 1 odds on the hard 6 and hard 8 and only 7 to 1 on the hard 4 and hard 10. These women believe that it is just as easy to make a double 3 as it is a double 5 and that the odds should therefore be the same against making either 6 or 10 the hard way. They see no reason why, if the house pays 9 to 1 against throwing a double 3 or a double 4, it shouldn't also be 9 to 1 against throwing a double 5 or a double 2.

The fallacy in the average woman gambler's reasoning is that when she makes the statement that it is just as easy to throw double 3's and double 4's as it is double 2's and double 5's, she seems to forget that she is talking about the hard way.

Suppose your point is 4 and you bet that you can make it the hard way with 2 and 2. There are, according to our table of Combinations and Ways, three ways to make 4, with 2 and 2, 1 and 3, and 3 and 1. If either 1 and 3 or 3 and 1 is thrown, you have made your point; but, since you didn't make it the hard way, you lose the bet. You have one way to win and two ways to lose. In addition, you can also lose if you 7 out; and since there are six ways to make 7, there are altogether eight ways you can lose as against one way in which you can win. Consequently, the odds are 8 to 1. The same reasoning also applies to making the point 10 with 5 and 5.

Let's try the same process with points 6 and 8: 6, according to the Combination and Ways table, can be made in five ways. Betting on the 6 the hard way means that only one of these ways (3 and 3) wins and the other four lose. Add to those the six losing ways that 7 can be made, and you have ten ways to lose against one way to win. The odds, therefore—strange as it may seem to players who don't think logically—are 10 to 1. The same reasoning applies to making 8 with 4 and 4.

One-Roll or Come-Out Bets: And now we come to the last of the foolish side bets that can be made on the Craps layout, the "One-Roll," or "Come-Out," bets. Strange as it may appear, these bets are made by smart-money gamblers and chump players alike. Gamblers who like their action fast and sweet and those who like their odds big, go for these bets the way Reds flock to riots. Like the Field bet, these bets are wagered on one roll, or throw, of the dice. The player bets that a specific number will be made. The dice are rolled, and the bet is won or lost on that roll.

a) 12 (two 6's) in one roll: The house pays 30 to 1; and since the correct odds are 35 to 1, the house has an edge of 13⅛ percent or about 69 cents on a $5 wager. When the house pays 30 for 1, it has an edge of 16⅔ percent, or about 83 cents on a $5 wager.

b) 2 (two aces) in one roll: house odds and percentages are the same as for the two 6's.

c) 11 (6 and 5) in one roll: The house pays 15 to 1; and since the correct odds are 17 to 1, the house has an edge of 11⅑ percent, or about 56 cents on a $5 wager. When the house pays 15 for 1, it has an edge of 16⅔ percent, or about 83 cents on a $5 wager.

d) 3 (1 and 2) in one roll: house odds and percentages are the same as for 11.

e) All 7's (3 and 4, 5 and 2, or 6 and 1) in one roll: The house pays either 5 for 1 or 4 to 1; and since the correct odds are 5 to 1, the house has an edge of 16⅔ percent, or about 83 cents on a $5 wager, which makes this and the four bets described above the biggest sucker bets found on the Bank Craps layout.

f) Any crap (2, 3, or 12) in one roll: The house pays 8 for 1 or 7 to 1; and since the correct odds are 8 to 1, the house has an edge of 11⅑ percent, or 56 cents on a $5 wager.

Now we come to the most popular betting system at Craps, known as "buying insurance."

Insurance Bets: Many women crapshooters have a habit of making two wagers simultaneously in an attempt to insure one or the other. For example, a woman places a bet on the Pass Line, and tries to protect it against a crap on the first roll by making a come-out bet on All Craps.

She thinks that if she loses one bet she may win the other, thus cutting down or canceling out her loss, when actually she stands to lose at least one of the bets and maybe both. Or she may attempt to insure a Don't Pass Line bet after the come-out by taking odds on the point. Since every wager in Bank Craps must be considered as a separate and distinct wager, the only effect of insurance betting is simply to pay the house a toll on two bets rather than on one. Instead of insuring herself against loss, the player has merely increased the percentage against herself.

And now I give you Scarne's Bank Craps Betting System, a method of betting at Bank Craps used by the nation's outstanding male smart-money gamblers, including The late Nick

The Greek, one of America's most famous gamblers, who was, by the way, a "Don't Bettor":

SCARNE'S BANK CRAPS BETTING SYSTEM

RULES FOR THE DO BETTOR

1. Bet the Pass Line.
2. Whenever possible, take the free odds in an amount equal to your Pass Line bet.
3. Bet the Come.
4. Whenever possible, take the free odds in an amount equal to your Come bet.
5. Make as few bets as possible, because the more bets you make, the less are your chances of winning.
6. Stay away from proposition and side bets.

RULES FOR THE DON'T BETTOR

1. Bet the Don't Pass Line.
2. Whenever possible, lay the free odds in an amount equal to your Don't Pass Line bet.
3. Bet the Don't Come.
4. Whenever possible, lay the free odds in an amount equal to your Don't Come bet.
5. Make as few bets as possible, because the more bets you make, the less are your chances of winning.
6. Stay away from proposition and side bets.

The above-described system is not expected to beat the house. Like all other betting systems, the user is bucking adverse odds, and eventually must lose. But what it does do is to cut down the house's earning power to a rock-bottom minimum of less than 1 percent—thereby bettering your chances of walking away from the dice table a winner. But this I'll guarantee—no other method or system of Craps betting equals it.

So that the reader can familiarize herself with the Bank Craps layout, and see at a glance each bet's payoff odds and favorable house percentage, the following illustration has been designed especially for this book:

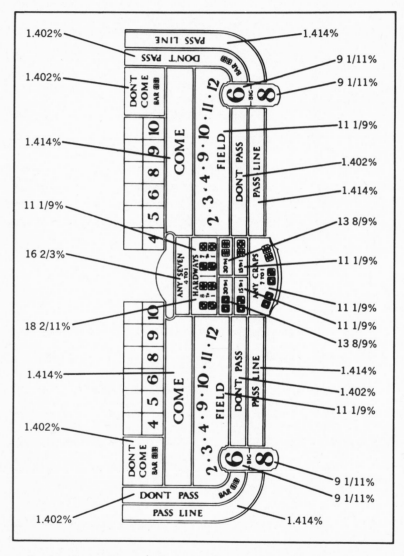

Banks Craps layout, showing the percentage takes of the house on various bets

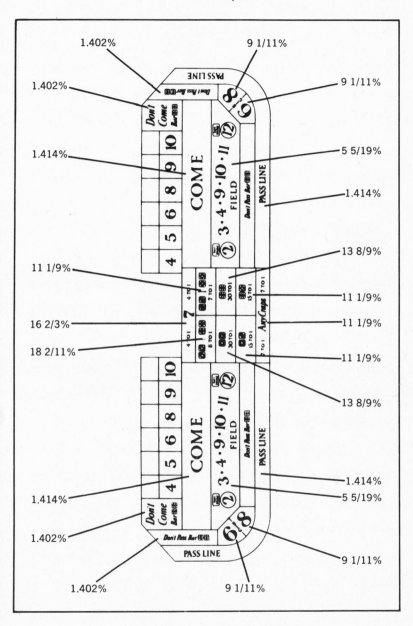

Alternate Bank Craps layout

4

Blackjack, B.J., or Twenty-one

It is a matter of record that this game is the most widely played and most fascinating banking card game in the world. Blackjack is played in every casino, private cardroom, or gaming club from California to New England and from New York to Panama. Every major casino in Nevada, Panama, Puerto Rico, Bonaire, and in the Grand Bahamas harbors at least five Blackjack tables.

My survey shows that about 21 million Americans, of whom 8 million are women, play Blackjack in one or more gambling casinos each year. This figure shows an increase of 2 million women Blackjack players since 1960. Although men still outnumber women Blackjack players 13 to 8, so many more women are playing the game each year that it will not surprise me if the number of women players surpasses that of the men in the next five years.

There is almost as sharp a scholarly dispute over the origin of Blackjack as there is over that of Poker. Italy and France have claimed it as their own, the French alleging a blood relationship with their Baccarat or Chemin de Fer (Shimmy), the Italians insisting that it is a vulgarization of their Seven and a Half. The games are obviously similar structurally. The American edition of Hoyle of 1875 calls it Vingt-Un. Foster's Hoyle, thirty years later in date, lists it as Vingt-et-Un. Today a substantial number of Englishmen still call the game Vanjohn or Pontoon. From Vingt-Un to Vingt-et-Un to Vanjohn to Pontoon to Blackjack to B.J. (as casino employees call it) it's still essentially the same game.

It must be understood at the beginning that this chapter is primarily concerned with the game of Blackjack as it is now played in gambling casinos the world over. The primary difference between the casino game and the private game of Blackjack that is played at home among friends is that in the private or friendly game every player has the right and opportunity to become dealer and banker. In the casino type of game the house does all the dealing and all the banking of the game.

Before I continue, I must warn my women readers not to fall for the misleading Blackjack information contained in two recently published gambling books whose authors promise their readers that if they follow their Blackjack system of play they are sure to beat the casino Blackjack tables. These books are *Beat the Dealer,* by Professor Edward O. Thorp, a mathematician from New Mexico State University, and *The Casino Gambler's Guide,* written by Dr. Allan N. Wilson, a mathematician and computer programer. During the past few years the misleading information contained in these books was responsible for the loss by untold numbers of old and newly made women Blackjack players of their hard-earned cash at the B.J. tables in Nevada, Puerto Rico, and elsewhere. I know because I have personally witnessed dozens of women Blackjack players during the past several years go broke playing one or the other of these so-called "infallible" systems.

In brief, contrary to the writings of these scientists, casino Blackjack cannot legitimately be beaten either by Professor Thorp, Dr. Wilson, or any of their system followers. Casino operators the world over have come to love Thorp and Wilson for increasing their Blackjack profits in the past few years. They pray daily that another Thorp or Wilson will soon come along with a so-called "infallible" system for beating Bank Craps or Roulette.

To prove my point, let me relate the following incident that occurred at a casino where I am the overseer, shortly after Wilson's volume hit the bookstores. Several women descended upon the Caribe Hilton Casino in Puerto Rico armed with small cards on which they had copied Wilson's Blackjack system. It amused the Blackjack dealers whenever they saw one of these women seated at the B.J. tables consult her card before making a decision. So much so, in fact, that whenever Miguel Amato, the casino manager, spotted the card consulters he would remark, "Thanks to Dr. Allan Wilson for bringing us these gullible women. Blackjack customers with lots of nice new, fresh American dollars."

One evening while I was standing in the casino's Blackjack pit, a woman whom I had just seen lose $1,500 while consulting Wilson's strategy card, entered the pit to cash a check. After introducing myself, I said, "I see it didn't do you any good to make use of Wilson's infallible Blackjack system."

"Mr. Scarne," she replied, "before reading Wilson's book, I knew nothing about Blackjack. The book was so convincing that I decided to become a Blackjack player and win some of that easy money Wilson spoke so much about. Then my vacation time arrived, and I decided to spend it in Puerto Rico because Blackjack playing is legal here. I had plans to win enough money at the tables to pay for my vacation. But instead, here I am, after a week's stay, a $2,000 Blackjack loser—thanks to Dr. Allan Wilson and his computer, which told him that even an amateur like me could beat the house."

Contrary to the views expressed by Thorp and Wilson, their so-called "infallible" systems favor the house, not the players.

The majority of the thousands of women that I have scouted playing Blackjack during the past fifteen years know little or nothing about the science of the game. The lack of such knowledge puts most of them in the chump, or sucker, category. In the following text I promise to tell the woman reader how she can stop being a chump and become as wise gambling at Blackjack as most of the professionals found in Puerto Rico, Nevada, or elsewhere. The following Blackjack information, if put to use, will do just that. However, before we begin our analysis of Blackjack strategy, you should learn the rules of the game. Although the basic rules of Blackjack as played in casinos the world over are the same, several minor variations do exist. For example, some Nevada casinos deal the game with a single deck from the hand. Others use either two or four decks dealt out of a miniature Chemin de Fer box, called a "shoe," which releases one card at a time face down. Puerto Rican casinos make use of two or four decks that are dealt out of a Chemin de Fer dealing box. Most Nevada casinos deal the player's first two cards face down; some deal them face up.

However, the rules to be discussed are the ones that I developed and first installed at the Caribe Hilton Hotel Casino back in late 1949. These rules are presently being used in most casinos in the Caribbean, Latin America and in a number of Nevada casinos. These rules and method of play in Blackjack have proved over the past fifteen years to be the best casino rules in use anywhere, not only for the Blackjack player but for the casino operator as well. I predict that in the near future my casino Blackjack rules will become standard in all gambling establishments throughout the world.

Let's move over to the Blackjack table at the Caribe Hilton Casino and watch a game as it gets under way. Four regulation decks of fifty-two playing cards each are seen individually spread face up ribbon-fashion across the table's surface. This procedure of card spreading is for the sole purpose of permitting players to see the cards before the play begins and to make certain that four standard decks of fifty-two cards each are in use and that no additional cards have been added or removed. A player takes a seat at the table, hands the B.J. dealer a $20 bill, and requests $1 chips. The dealer removes twenty $1 chips from the chip rack and places them in front of the player. The dealer, using a small paddle, pushes the paper money into a slot in the table, and it falls into a locked box beneath.

But, before the Blackjack action starts, let's give the table a once-over. The tabletop is half-moon shaped, approximately 6 feet long by 3½ feet wide, and accommodates from one to seven players who sit around the circular side of the table; the dealer stands opposite the players, directly in front of the chip rack. To the dealer's right you see a discard box, a receptacle in which the dead cards (cards that have been played) are placed as the game progresses. As you see, the table's surface is covered with a tight-fitting green baize cloth called the "layout." In the center of the layout are printed, in bold letters, the following basic rules, which are now standard in all major casinos in Nevada, Puerto Rico, Bonaire, Grand Bahamas, and elsewhere:

BLACKJACK
PAYS 3 TO 2
DEALER MUST DRAW TO 16 AND STAND ON 17

Next let's see how Blackjack is played at the Caribe Hilton Hotel Casino in San Juan, Puerto Rico.

The game is about to start, and as the dealer scoops up the four face-up decks that are spread across the tabletop. The dealer, after thoroughly shuffling the four decks together, hands a player a face-up joker and pushes the packet of 208 cards sideways toward the player and says, "Cut the cards, please." The player inserts the joker halfway into the packet when he wants the cards to be "cut." The dealer completes the cut by placing the bottom portion of the cut deck on top of the cut portion. He squares the cards and inserts a second face-up joker about 30 cards from the bottom of the 208-card packet.

The dealer then places the 208-card packet face down into a card box, withdraws the top card, shows it, and places it face up in the discard box and is ready to deal. When the joker makes its appearance (the joker the dealer himself inserted near the bottom of the quadruple deck), the deal ends, and the dealer must begin a new shuffle and again repeat the above-described procedure. In essence, the 30 bottom cards of the 208-card packet never come into actual play. This ruling was first devised by me back in 1948 to prevent any "case-down" or "countdown" player from memorizing the cards as they are being dealt and by so doing learn the identity of the last few undealt cards—thereby gaining an advantage over the house.

The player's first two cards, in addition to all others, are dealt face up at the Caribe Hilton Casino Blackjack tables. When the first two cards are dealt face up to a player, it helps the dealer to correct any errors that the player may have made when total-ing the numbered value of the player's hand. In addition, it prevents any card-cheat player from switching one or both of his or her face-down cards that he or she may have secretly palmed; and at the same time, owing to the fact that the dealer (house) does not have any discretionary power on when to hit or stand, it doesn't matter if the dealer sees the player's cards or not.

So that you will readily understand everything that takes place during the actual playing of a Blackjack game, here are the rules:

SCARNE'S RULES FOR CASINO BLACKJACK

The Object of the Game: A player tries to obtain a higher total card count than the dealer by reaching 21, or as close to 21 as possible, without exceeding that count. If the player's total count exceeds 21, she has "busted," lost her bet. The dealer immediately scoops up the lost bet and the dead cards, which he places face up in the discard box. The player, at her proper turn of play and at her own discretion, may stand, or draw one or more cards in an attempt to better her card count.

Value of the Cards: The cards have the following values: Aces count either 1 or 11, at the discretion of the holder. Kings, queens, and jacks have each a count of 10. All other cards, 2, 3, 4, 5, 6, 7, 8, 9, and 10, are counted at face value. The jokers do not enter the play. They are used only as indicators.

Betting: Before the deal begins, each player must place her chip or chips wager in the betting space, which is a rectangle painted on the playing surface directly before her and in full view of the dealer. Caribe Hilton Casino players can bet as many hands as the casino manager deems it best for the convenience of the other players. Blackjack tables at the Hilton Casino bear seven rectangular betting spaces. When a player plays more than one hand at a time, she must play the hand farthest to her right to completion before being permitted to play her next hand or hands.

The Deal: After all player's bets are down, the dealer, starting with the player on his extreme left, begins dealing clockwise, giving one card face up to each player and one face up to himself. He next deals each player a second face-up card and a second card face down to himself. This he slides under his face-up card. That ends the first phase of the deal.

The First Turn of Play: If the dealer's face-up card is a 10 count or an ace, he must look at his hole (face-down) card. If he has a natural 21 (count of 21 with 2 cards), he must face it and announce, "Twenty-One," or "Blackjack," and the deal comes to an end for all the players. Any player with a natural 21 also announces it, and the dealer declares this to be a "stand-

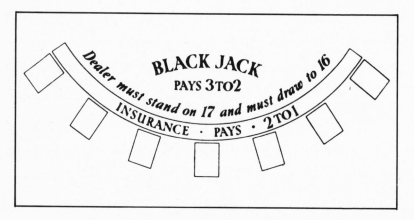

Layout of Blackjack table

off," or "push." There is no action on this player's hand. He neither wins nor loses. The dealer wins, and collects bets from all players having a lesser card count than 21. The dealer collects all the dead cards and places them in the discard box. Then he deals the next round.

But if the dealer's face-up card is an ace, before looking at his face-down card he must announce a call for insurance. A player who desires insurance against the dealer having a natural (21) places an amount equal to half of her present wager in the betting rectangle directly in front of her. When all players have had an opportunity of placing an insurance bet, the dealer then peeks at his face-down card. If it is a 10-count card, giving him Blackjack, he turns it face up and pays all insurance bets 2-to-1 odds. But if the dealer's face-down card is not a 10 count, he collects the amounts wagered on insurance, and the hand continues to be played as follows:

When the dealer does not hold a natural 21, he scans each player's two face-up cards and pays off all players holding a natural 21 at 3-to-2 odds. This means that if a player has bet $2 she collects $5—her own $2 plus an additional $3. The dealer then scoops up all the dead cards and places them in the discard box.

Then, starting with the player at his extreme left, the play continues as follows: If the two cards total less than 21, she may elect: (*a*) To stand—either she is satisfied with her count or fears that a third card may make her count go over 21. She says, "Good," or, "I have enough," or, "I stay"; or she signifies that she is standing simply by sliding her cards under the chip or chips she has bet; (*b*) To draw a card or cards when a player is not satisfied with her count, and says, "Hit me," or makes a beckoning motion by closing and opening her hand, or a come-on motion with a finger. The dealer then deals another card off the top of the deck face up before the player and next to her original two cards.

Although the cards are dealt one at a time, the player may continue to draw as many as she likes. When she believes the count to be the best she can get, she stays. If she draws a card that puts her count over 21, the dealer announces "bust," and scoops up the player's bet and cards and places the dead cards in the discard box. The play then moves to the player's left, clockwise, around the table, until all players have played out their hands.

The Second Turn of Play: If all players have busted, the dealer merely places his own two unplayed cards in the discard box and deals a new hand. If one or more players with a count of 21 or less remain, the dealer must play out his hand. He turns up his face-down card so that his two cards are now exposed. If his total card count is 17, 18, 19, or 20, the dealer must stand; he is not permitted to draw a card. If his count is 16 or less, he must draw a card, and continue to draw until his count reaches 17 or more—at which point he must stand. Thus the dealer has no options whatsoever at his disposal, and from his standpoint Blackjack is strictly a mechanical game. If the dealer draws one or more cards, and busts, he must pay off the players still in the game. If the dealer holds a "soft" 17, that is, a 17 count that includes an ace, he must also stand. This also applies to a soft 18, 19, or 20. It is important to repeat here that the Blackjack dealer has no choice as to whether he should stand or draw. His decisions are predetermined and known to the players in advance. Since all the dealer's cards are exposed at his turn of play, he has no opportunity for any departure from these rules. The rule requiring the dealer to hit on 16 or less and stay on 17, 18, 19, 20, and 21 is standard today in all casinos here and abroad.

Final Settlement: At the end of his play the dealer starts with the first active player on his right and moves around the table counterclockwise, paying off the players who have a higher count than his with an amount equal to the bet they placed, and collecting the placed bets from players showing a lesser count, and at the same time scooping up each player's dead cards. If the dealer busts, he pays off each surviving active player with an amount equal to her bet.

Splitting Pairs: Any player whose first two dealt cards are of identical value, that is, any pair (two 3's, two 4's and so on) may split the pair and treat each card as the first card dealt in two separate hands by separating her two cards and betting the same amount on each hand as she had on her original hand. When pairs are split, the player's original bet is placed on one of these cards, and an equal amount must be bet on the other. The player is then dealt one face-up card on the face-up card on her right, and she must play this hand out. If, in drawing to the first face-up card, she forms a pair again, she may again split pairs, betting an amount equal to her original wager on this third hand. She may continue to split any additional pairs. The first hand on the player's extreme right must be played to completion before the adjacent split hand is dealt a second card. Each split hand must be played to completion in its proper order from the player's right to her left.

Double Down: When the player's first two dealt cards total a count of 11, the player may elect to double the amount of her bet and draw one additional card, which will be dealt face down. The player must not look at this card until the dealer turns his hole card face up. This is known as "double down."

Most Nevada casinos deal the player's first two cards face down, and permit a double down on any two cards. In addition some Las Vegas Strip casinos, such as The Sands and The Dunes, permit a second double down on a count of 9 if a player draws a 2 as her first double-down card. The El Casino in the Grand Bahamas permits doubling down on counts of 9, 10, and 11 only.

I suggest to the reader who plans to try her luck at Blackjack to learn the casino rules backward and forward. This can be done simply by consulting your dealer. Casino Blackjack rules are easy to remember. If you do not have a complete understanding of rules of play where you gamble, you suffer a serious percentage handicap even before you make your first bet.

In the following pages I shall show you exactly where the house extracts its advantage, and how you can shave that percentage to a minimum. But, more important, if you adhere to my strategy, you will certainly improve your game, and become as Blackjack-sharp as most professional gamblers in Las Vegas or Puerto Rico.

In Blackjack, the house advantage is the result of the dealer playing last. When you bust by going over the mathematical deadline of 21, the dealer doesn't bother to wait to play his hand. He rakes in your bet, and as far as you are concerned the transaction is closed. You are through. All you can do is sit around and wait until the hand is completed and a new deal takes place.

This is the crux of the hidden percentage that works in the house's favor; this is the real reason why gambling-house operators get richer and players, poorer.

For this is the only casino game in which you are gambling against two opponents at the same time. Your first opponent is the dealer; against him you are trying merely to win the house's money. The second opponent is the player herself. Every woman drives herself to see how close—how much closer (hit me again)—she can get to 21. And the Blackjack fancier's most merciless opponent is herself. How often has this happened to you? You get a 15 on your first two cards. It's not the sort of count a woman of your type likes to stand on. You're not content with a drab, mushy little 15! Never.

"Hit me," you say, and pray for a 6 and get a 9 or a King. You bust, and the dealer scoops up your bet. But did the dealer beat you? Did he beat your count? Don't be silly; you've beaten yourself. One more thing—if your prayers are accorded due notice in Heaven, and you draw your 6, have you won? Hell, no! You still have the dealer to beat.

The dealer has the advantage, then, in the unspoken provision that he plays last.

However, this isn't so unfair as it may appear, because the dealer has several disadvantages going against him. These house disadvantages will help reduce the dealer's advantage of playing last—that is, providing the player knows what to do. The big disadvantages the dealer has are that even when he sees your cards and knows you're standing with a 12, 13, 14, or 15, and he holds 16, he must hit. On the other hand, if you hold a count of 18, 19, 20, or 21, and he has 17, he must stand. Another dealer's liability is the fact that one of the dealer's first two cards is dealt face up. This, combined with the dealer's predetermined rules of drawing to 16 or less and standing on 17 or more, is going to figure prominently in the strategy I have outlined in the following pages.

The majority of women Blackjack players I have seen in action fail to consider these dealer disadvantages. They play the same type of game regardless of the value of the dealer's face-up card. If you are one of those B.J. players who refuse to hit a possible bust hand (12, 13, 14, 15, 16), take insurance, split pairs, and double down without any reason whatever, Lady, I have news for you—you are Blackjack's biggest sucker because you may be fighting a disadvantage that runs from 7 to 12 percent or more. If you are one of those B.J. players who mimic the dealer by continuously hitting a possible bust hand (12, 13, 14, 15, 16) and never split pairs, double down, or take insurance, you are considerably better off than the lady above. However, you're still fighting an average 6 percent. If you're a hunch player who hits, stands, splits pairs, and doubles down whenever the urge strikes you, sister, who knows how outlandish a house percentage you're actually bucking?

If you adhere to the strategy that I shall outline for you in the following pages, I promise that you can cut down the house's advantage to an average of 3 percent. My evidence comes from the playing and clocking of tens of thousands of expertly played hands in a half-dozen casinos during the past fifteen years.

The strategy I shall outline utilizes these factors: the fact that the dealer must hit 16 or less and stand on 17 or more; the knowledge of the dealer's face-up (exposed) card; the player's total count; and when it is to your advantage to stand, to draw, to split pairs, and double down.

Playing according to the tables listed below will assure you that you are fighting an average house advantage of 3 percent instead of those outlandish big percentages that most women

Blackjack players try to beat. However, my strategy does not guarantee that you will win—it simply cuts down the house percentage to its lowest possible level, and gives you a much better opportunity to win than any other method of Blackjack play.

SCARNE'S BASIC STRATEGY RULES FOR BLACKJACK

Hitting and Standing on Hard Counts

1. When the dealer's upcard is anything, stand on a count of 17 or more.
2. When the dealer's upcard is anything, draw to a count of 2 to 11.
3. When the dealer's upcard is a 5-spot or 6-spot, the player should stand on a count of 12 or more.
4. When the dealer's upcard is a 2-, 3-, or 4-spot, the player should stand on a count of 13 or more.
5. When the dealer's upcard is an Ace or 10-count card, the player should stand on a count of 16 or more.
6. When the dealer's upcard is a 7-, 8-, or 9-spot, the player should hit a count of 16 or less.

Soft-Hand Strategy

When a player holds a hand that contains an ace, there are sometimes two possible counts, neither of which exceeds 21. A hand containing an ace and a 6 may have a count, or value, of either 7 or 17, because an ace can be valued as either 1 or 11. This ambiguous type of hand is known to Blackjack dealers as a soft count or a two-way hand. Playing it correctly requires special strategic considerations, as follows:

1. When the dealer's upcard is an 8, 9, 10, or ace, the player should stand only on a soft 19 or higher.
2. When the dealer's upcard is either a 2, 3, 4, 5, 6, or 7 count, the player should stand only on a soft 18 or higher.

Note that the holder of a soft hand should never stand until her total count is at least 18. She should continue to draw to her soft count, and stand as indicated above. If, when the player draws one or more cards, her soft count exceeds 21 (this occurs often, since a high soft count is being hit), the player should revert to the standard hard-count hit-or-stand strategy because she no longer holds a soft hand.

Example: The dealer's upcard is a 6-spot; the player hits a soft 14 and draws a 9-spot. Her total count is now 13. If she counts the ace as 11, she has a count of 23. The hand is no longer soft, so the player reverts to her standard strategy, and stands on 13.

Soft hands are advantageous to the player because if she uses the right strategy she gets two chances: first she tries for a high count by hitting a soft count, and if that fails she reverts to the standard hard-count hit-and-draw strategy.

Splitting Pairs

1. Never split 4's, 5's, 6's, or 9's.
2. Always split 8's unless the dealer's upcard is a 9- or 10-spot.
3. Split 7's when the dealer's upcard is a 5, 6, or 7.
4. Always split aces, even when the casino rules permit only a 1-card draw to a split ace.
5. Always split 10-count cards when the dealer's upcard is a 5 or 6.

Doubling Down

1. Always double down on a count of 11, no matter what the value of the dealer's upcard is.
2. Double down on a count of 10 when the dealer's upcard is anything but a 10 count.
3. Double down on a count of 9 when the dealer's upcard is a 2, 3, 4, 5, or 6.
4. Double down on a soft 12, 13, 14, 15, 16, or 17 when the dealer's upcard is a 6.

The strategy rules shown above take into consideration all the Blackjack bets permitted in all the casinos the world over.

However, rarely will you find a casino in which you put into play all strategy rules described above. Example: Casinos in Puerto Rico permit a double down on 11 only. Bud Sweet's Bonaire Casino permits a double down on 9, 10, and 11 only. The Sands Hotel Casino in Las Vegas permits a double down on any two cards. And so it goes from casino to casino. However, the hit-and-stand strategy rules on both the hard and soft counts are usable in all casinos, and will be of greater help in cutting down the house's advantage than all the other strategies combined. So, memorize them first.

Insurance Betting

Some casinos allow players to make a so-called insurance bet against losing to a natural whenever the dealer shows an ace as his upcard. Since the insurance bet pays off at 2-to-1 odds, the player must win one-third of the time to get a dead-even proposition. If the dealer's upcard is an ace, and you have no knowledge of any other cards, then the dealer's down card may be considered drawn at random from 51 cards that remain unseen. But under such conditions the 51-card deck contains 16 10-count cards, and the player can win this bet only when the dealer has a 10-count card in the hole. In the long run she will win only 16 of her bets, losing 35. Since insurance bets are paid off at 2 to 1, or 32 to 16 against an expectation of 35 to 16, the player is shorted $\frac{3}{51}$, or approximately 6 percent, or, to be exact, $5\frac{15}{17}$ percent.

Most women gamblers unwisely insist on buying insurance whenever they hold Blackjack on the grounds that they want to be sure of a win. The odds are 34 to 15 the dealer doesn't have a natural, and you will not receive the 2-to-1 insurance odds. Your expectation is minus $\frac{4}{49}$ for a house edge of about 8 percent.

As a general rule I don't recommend insurance betting for women. However, the casual card caser (counter) can use the insurance bet advantageously if she has kept track of the 10-count cards dealt in previous hands. For example, suppose half the deck (26 cards) has been dealt and the card caser recalls that only three 10-count cards have been dealt. If an insurance bet could be made on the next deal, it would be wise to take out insurance. Under these circumstances the player will win $1\frac{3}{26}$, or 50 percent, of her bets. Since the bank pays insurance bets off at 2 to 1, the player has an edge of $33\frac{1}{3}$ percent over the bank on this bet.

For the above reason banks permit players to bet only half the amount of their initial wager when making an insurance bet, and for the same reason many casinos no longer permit any insurance bets.

But don't think for a moment that card casing and the memorizing of previously dealt cards will put the Blackjack percentages in your favor—not with the present-day method of dealing casino Blackjack.

I have known only six professional male gamblers and one woman in my entire gambling history who ever beat the game of Blackjack by putting the percentages in their favor through "card casing," or, as it is more commonly known, "counting down the deck." I was the first person to beat the game with a countdown, and the first to be barred from playing Blackjack in Las Vegas, back in 1947. I was barred because I told Benjamin (Bugsy) Siegal, owner of the swank Flamingo Hotel Casino, that I could beat the game with a countdown. He challenged me to prove it. I did by beating every casino on the Las Vegas Strip. The result—I was barred from the casino Blackjack tables throughout Nevada and the rest of the country.

Though card casing, or counting down the deck, has been a lost gimmick since 1955, now and then you'll spot a Johnny Come Lately trying it on some casino boss. If the boss doesn't know his business, the card caser may get away with it.

The machinations of a modern-day card caser stand out like a bright light in a moonless night. First, he seeks a vacant B.J. table for himself. Then his stooge, who is a partial card caser, takes his position beside him—sometimes he makes use of two stooges. At the beginning of each new deal, his bets are usually the house minimum on each of the six or seven betting spaces.

This type of betting continues until near the end of each deal, when a whispered consultation takes place between the card caser and his assistants. If they agree that the remaining un-dealt cards appear disadvantageous to the house, they increase the size of their bets to the maximum house limit. A smart house man counters this B.J. chicanery by reshuffling the entire deck, including the undealt cards. The card caser complains a bit, calls off his bets, exits from the casino, and shops around seeking a casino whose boss is stupid enough to stand for such nonsense. That's the life of a professional card caser. Most of these casers haven't got a dime. Therefore my advice is: Don't try to be a card caser.

However, one point I should like to emphasize is that an important practice to follow at the Blackjack tables is that when your luck is running good, and you're winning money, by all means increase the size of your bets and try to win as much as possible in the shortest space of time. However, if your luck is running bad, decrease the size of your bets. Better yet, seek the nearest exit.

5

Roulette

Roulette, the glamour banking game that made Monte Carlo the world's most famous casino, is today the favorite gambling pastime of some 10,000,000 American women. Visit any casino in the United States, Puerto Rico, or the Caribbean islands, and you will find on the average that four out of six players seated at a Roulette table are women. Roulette has an aura of glamour that makes it especially attractive to women. When a woman enters a casino for the first time, it is almost a sure bet that, after playing the slot machines, the first game she tries will be Roulette. Why? Because the word Roulette itself brings to a woman's mind plush casinos, millionaire playboys, kings, princes, beautiful women, flamboyant bets, and enormous fortunes won and lost overnight.

In addition, Roulette combines a number of elements that make it the ideal casino game for women. To begin with, it's very easy to play. Second, it's a game where big winnings build up quickly, and two straight number hits, each of which pay off at odds of 35 to 1, are equivalent to the winnings of seventy constant Pass or Don't Pass Line bets at the Bank Craps table. It is a game where a woman's favorite lucky number is a very real, very romantic factor. It is the casino's number-one spectator sport—when a high bettor gets hot, a crowd forms, tension fills the air, and everybody is as excited as the hot bettor herself. All these factors are what make the game of Roulette so fascinating for women.

Roulette is a game that every woman feels she has to try at least once when she visits a casino in Nevada, Puerto Rico, or elsewhere. To most women its appealing quality is that it is a relaxing game—that is, unless she happens to be a Roulette addict who spends the time in between spins placing wagers all over the betting layout. Roulette is undoubtedly the most cultured of all casino games; contrary to the views expressed by most of our present-day gambling writers, it gives the average woman gambler as good an overall run for her money as Bank Craps or Blackjack. In addition, Roulette offers as wide a variety of bets as any other casino game, including Bank Craps, yet the slower pace and simpler rules of play make it a much easier game for the average woman gambler to enjoy. To this add the fact that it offers the woman gambler whose budget is modest an opportunity to gamble for a long while with a small investment.

Roulette, however, has its share of reckless, big-time women gamblers. The most notable one I ever saw in action was a Las Vegas showgirl, a girl friend of a high-rolling Midwestern gambler.

Early one Sunday morning in December, 1958, at Mike and Bill McLaney's Nacional Hotel Casino in Havana, just one year before the bearded Communist Fidel Castro took over Cuba, I stopped in to say hello to the McLaney brothers, and as we exchanged handshakes, Mike said: "Scarne, follow me. I want you to watch the fastest high-rolling woman gambler in Havana. She's already beaten me for $65,000 in the past four nights. Look over at that roulette table." He nodded toward an attractive lone brunette at a nearby roulette table whom I recognized as Peggy _____, a Las Vegas showgirl. Mike continued:

"You'll notice she always bets the $100 maximum house limit on the four corners, four splits, and the straight numbers—and she makes it a habit to bet the same three numbers—5, 23, and 32. Somehow we can't seem to beat her."

As I watched in amazement, Peggy kept boxing her favorite three numbers with $100 black chips for a total wager of $2,700 on each spin of the wheel. On several occasions when the little ivory ball dropped into Peggy's winning number and the croupier pushed her $13,500 worth of black chips, I studied Peggy's reactions, and noticed that she didn't even crack a faint smile while raking in her counters. She wore the same poker-faced expression, win or lose.

It was seven o'clock in the morning, and at that hour the casino was empty with the exception of Peggy, her croupier, Mike and Bill McLaney, and myself, when Peggy turned to Mike McLaney and said, "Mike, I'm a $42,000 winner tonight—how about increasing your $100 single-number limit to $1,000 for me? I'm tired, and I'd like to play the same three numbers for about fifteen minutes more. Are you game, Mike?"

Mike threw Bill and me a quizzical stare, then turned to Peggy, looked her straight in the eyes, and asked, "Peggy, do you know what you're saying? It will cost you $27,000 a spin!"

"Yes, Mike, I do. But if the 5, 23, or 32 hits, you'll owe me an additional $117,000," replied Peggy in a matter-of-fact manner.

Mike caught a nod from his brother-partner Bill, then said: "Peggy, it's a deal. You have a $1,000-limit on the corners, splits, and straight numbers."

Peggy nodded as she impassively watched the busy croupier ring each of the numbers 5, 23, and 32 with nine $1,000 markers. She had $27,000 riding on the next spin of the wheel, the biggest sum I ever saw bet on one spin of a Roulette wheel.

After the croupier had finished boxing the numbers, he slowly spun the wheel in a counterclockwise direction, and as silence filled the air he sent the little ivory ball spinning on the wheel's back track. As the ball circled the back track, I studied Peggy's facial expression—it was as motionless as the face of a department-store dummy. As the whirling ball began to slow down, I could feel the tension growing around me. Seconds later the ball dropped from the back track and bounced several times over the bottom section of the spinning wheel and seemed to come to a dead stop in Number 5. "Wow!" shouted Peggy, but before she could utter another word the ball leaped out of Number 5 and came to rest in the adjacent pocket, Number 17.

As the croupier called 17, and pointed his index finger to Number 17 on the layout, Peggy rose from the table shaking her head, flashed a forced smile, and said, "Mike, cash me out; my luck has left me."

Peggy collected her $15,000 night's winnings and left the casino without saying good night. Minutes later, the McLaney boys heaved a loud sigh of relief and said, almost in unison, "Scarne, that dame is bound to give us ulcers, the way she bets the wheel."

On one of my recent fact-finding missions to Nevada, concerning women gamblers, I dropped in to see Mike and Bill McLaney at the Carousel Casino in downtown Las Vegas. As the conversation turned to Peggy's Havana Roulette escapade, Mike remarked, "Scarne, Peggy returned to Havana just once after beating us for 80 grand, and she told me that she had invested her $80,000 Roulette winnings in a trust fund and had quit gambling."

As I was leaving the Carousel, I told Mike and Bill, "Now we know of at least one Roulette player who beat the game."

So you'll understand everything about the structure, science, and rules of play concerning Roulette, let's walk over to a table situated in a Las Vegas Strip casino and allow me to explain the game to you. You'll notice that the table is composed of two sections—the wheel itself and the players' betting spaces —better known as the Roulette layout. The wheel itself: the only moving part consists of a solid wooden disk, slightly convex in shape. Around its bottom rim are metal partitions known as separators, and the compartments between these are called pockets. These pockets are metal, painted alternately red and black, except for two pockets that are green. Each of the red and black pockets bears a number from 1 to 36 in gold. The green pockets carry the signs 0 and 00, also in gold. With these two exceptions, the odd and even numbers and the high and low numbers run alternately, but not consecutively. Each number, color, and sign 0 and 00 on the wheel has its counterpart on the betting layout.

The standard Roulette table employs 5, 6, or 7 sets of chips. Each set is differently colored; each consists of 300 chips; and there is one set for each player. Chips are valued at 10 cents, 25 cents, 50 cents, $1, $5, $25, and $100. The values of the lower chip denominations, from 10 cents to $1 (unlike other casino chips) are not marked on them. The player must buy a minimum stack of 20 chips from the croupier (dealer), specifying the value she wishes to place on each chip and paying for them accordingly. The player then receives chips of a color different from those of the other players. She must cash them in when she leaves the table.

The maximum amounts permitted to be wagered on different spaces of the betting layout vary in Nevada and Caribbean casinos. However, the minimum bet allowed usually involves four minimum-value chips. For example, when playing 25-cent chips the player must bet a minimum of four chips on each spin of the wheel, although the four chips can be spread over the numbers on the layout as she desires, excluding bets that pay off at even money and 2 to 1, such as wagers placed on black, red, odd and even numbers, dozens (first 12, second 12, third 12), and vertical columns of the layout (each column containing twelve numbers). A minimum of four chips or a bet valued at $1 is required on all even-money or 2-to-1 bets. Many Strip casinos in Las Vegas permit a maximum of a $50 bet on a single or straight number. Puerto Rico's casinos, whose wagers are standardized by law, permit a maximum of only $10 on all betting spaces of the layout with the exception of even-money and 2-to-1 wagers, where the limit is $180.

To play the game, each player places her bets on the layout in any manner permitted by the rules. The croupier starts the wheel spinning in a counterclockwise direction, then flips the ball onto the wheel's back track so that it travels clockwise. Players may continue placing bets while wheel and ball are in motion until the croupier calls, "No more bets!" He does this as the ball slows down and is about to fall off the back track.

When the ball comes to rest in one of the pockets on the wheel, the croupier announces the winning color and number as he points with his index finger to the corresponding number on the betting layout. He then rakes in the losses and pays off the winners. It's as simple as that.

You can bet on a single number (including 0 and 00), a combination of numbers, the colors red, black, or green, or the odd and even numbers. The 0 and 00 are usually referred to as "house numbers" for the obvious reason that when the ball drops into either of these pockets the house wins all bets— except those that were wagered on 0 and 00.

As we can see from the betting layout, there are an equal number of red, black, odd, and even numbers—18 of each. A win on either one pays the winner even money (1 to 1). If we did not consider the house numbers 0 and 00, the probability of red, black, odd, or even winning would be fifty-fifty. However, the 0 and 00 must be considered, and here is where the house percentage comes into the picture. All wagers placed at the Roulette table with the exception of the Five-Number bet (explained later) amounts to a house advantage of $5\frac{5}{19}$ percent.

Here is how it is calculated: The player places her bet on a space of the layout marked black, red, odd, or even. She is betting that one of 18 numbers will win. There are, however, 18 numbers, plus the 0 and 00, for a total of 20 numbers, that will lose for her. Therefore the house's average gain will be 2 wins out of every 38 spins, so that its advantage is $\frac{2}{38}$ of 100, $5\frac{5}{19}$ percent, an average cost to the player of $5\frac{5}{19}$ cents of each dollar wagered.

Let's follow this reasoning a step further: Suppose you placed a chip bet on each of the 38 numbers (which includes the house numbers of 0 and 00). You would be sure to win because you covered all the numbers. But since you bet 38 chips, and received only 36 chips in winnings, you have lost 2 chips, or $\frac{2}{38}$ of 100, or $5\frac{5}{19}$ percent—an average money cost to you of $5\frac{5}{19}$ cents with each dollar bet.

Since Roulette betting layouts in America or the Caribbean do not vary as to bets permitted, odds offered, and percentages against the player, the following text covers all the bets permitted on any layout and the house's percentage advantage on each.

Straight Bet, or Single-Number Bet: The player places her chip(s) squarely on one number on the Roulette betting layout, making certain that the chip(s) do not touch any of the lines enclosing the number. This indicates that the player is betting that on the next spin of the wheel the little ivory ball will come to rest in the pocket of her number on the Roulette wheel. The house pays off at 35 to 1, pushing you a stack of 20 and a stack of 15 chips for each chip wagered, leaving your original wager on the layout as your next bet. Since the odds against are 37 to 1, the house's advantage is $5\frac{5}{19}$ percent.

The Signs 0 and 00: These can be played the same as any one of the 36 numbers. The house's favorable percentage is the same as on a Single-Number bet: $5\frac{5}{19}$ percent.

Split Bet, or Two-Number Bet: The player places her chip(s) directly on any horizontal or vertical line separating any two numbers on the betting layout. If the winning number is one of the two wagered on, the player wins and is paid off at 17-to-1 odds. Since the odds against are 18 to 1, the house's favorable advantage is $5\frac{5}{19}$ percent.

Street Bet, or Three-Number Bet: The player places her chip(s) on the outside vertical line of the betting layout. This indicates that she is betting the three numbers opposite the chip(s), across the layout. If the winning number is one of these three, the player wins and is paid off at odds of 11 to 1. Since the odds against are $11\frac{2}{3}$ to 1, the house's favorable advantage is $5\frac{5}{19}$ percent.

Square Bet, Quarter Bet, Corner Bet, or Four-Number Bet: The player places her chip(s) on the intersection of the lines touching any four numbers. If one of these four numbers wins, the player wins and is paid off at 8-to-1 odds. Since the odds against are 8½ to 1, the house's favorable edge is 5⁵⁄₁₉ percent.

Line Bet, or Five-Number Bet: The player places her chip(s) on the line separating the 1, 2, 3 from the 0 and 00 spaces at a corner intersection. This indicates that she is betting that one of the five numbers 1, 2, 3, 0, or 00 will win. If one of these five numbers wins, the player is paid off at odds of 6 to 1. Since the odds against are 6⅗ to 1, the house's favorable advantage is 7¹⁷⁄₁₉ percent.

Note that the house percentage differs from the 5⁵⁄₁₉ percent that is the bank's edge on all other Roulette bets. From the player's viewpoint, therefore, it is a bet to avoid because it has an additional disadvantage of 2¹²⁄₁₉ percent against the player as compared to all other Roulette bets.

Line Bet, or Six-Number Bet: The player places her chip(s) on the intersection of the vertical sideline and a horizontal line between two "streets." This indicates she is betting the three numbers above and the three numbers below the line on which the chip(s) are resting. If any of these six numbers wins, the player is paid off at odds of 5 to 1. Since the odds against are 5⅓ to 1, the house's favorable advantage is 5⁵⁄₁₉ percent.

Column Bet, or Twelve-Number Bet: The player places her chip(s) on one of the three blank spaces at the bottom of the layout. (Some layouts have three squares marked "1st," "2nd," "3rd.") This indicates that the player is betting the twelve vertical numbers above the space wagered on. If one of these twelve numbers wins, the player is paid off at 2-to-1 odds. Since the odds against are 2⅙ to 1, the house's favorable advantage is 5⁵⁄₁₉ percent.

Dozens, or Twelve-Number, Bet: The player places her chip(s) on one of the spaces of the betting layout marked "1st 12," "2nd 12," or "3rd 12." The 1st 12 indicates that the player is betting on the numbers 1 to 12 inclusive; the 2nd 12, the numbers 13 to 24 inclusive; and the 3rd 12, the numbers 25 to 36 inclusive. If one of the twelve numbers wagered on wins,

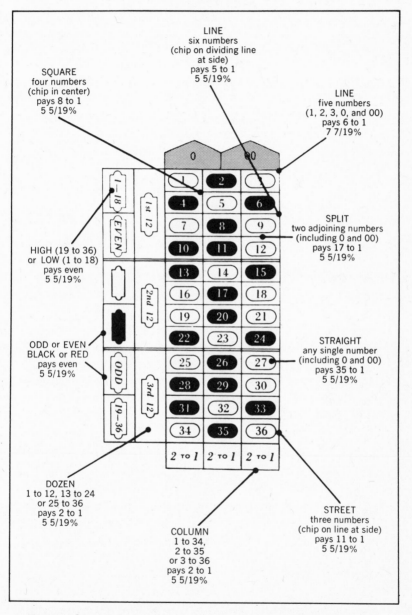

SQUARE
four numbers
(chip in center)
pays 8 to 1
5 5/19%

LINE
six numbers
(chip on dividing line
at side)
pays 5 to 1
5 5/19%

LINE
five numbers
(1, 2, 3, 0, and 00)
pays 6 to 1
7 7/19%

HIGH (19 to 36)
or LOW (1 to 18)
pays even
5 5/19%

SPLIT
two adjoining numbers
(including 0 and 00)
pays 17 to 1
5 5/19%

ODD or EVEN
BLACK or RED
pays even
5 5/19%

STRAIGHT
any single number
(including 0 and 00)
pays 35 to 1
5 5/19%

DOZEN
1 to 12, 13 to 24
or 25 to 36
pays 2 to 1
5 5/19%

COLUMN
1 to 34,
2 to 35
or 3 to 36
pays 2 to 1
5 5/19%

STREET
three numbers
(chip on line at side)
pays 11 to 1
5 5/19%

Betting layout for placement of chips in Roulette, together with percentage takes of the house on various bets the player is paid off at 2-to-1 odds, like the column bet described above. The correct odds are 2⅙ to 1. The house's advantage is 5⁵⁄₁₉ percent.

Low-Number Bet (1 to 18): The player places her chip(s) on the betting layout marked 1 to 18, which indicates that she is betting on the numbers 1 to 18 inclusive. If one of these numbers wins, the player is paid off at even money (1 to 1). The correct odds are 1⅑ to 1. The house's advantage is 5⁵⁄₁₉ percent.

High-Number Bet (19 to 36): The player places her chip(s) on the space of the betting layout marked 19 to 36, which indicates that she is betting on the numbers 19 to 36 inclusive. If one of these 18 numbers wins, the player is paid off at even money (1 to 1). The correct odds are 1⅑ to 1. The house's advantage is 5⁵⁄₁₉ percent.

Black-Color Bet: The player places her chip(s) on a space of the layout marked "Black." (Some layouts have a large black diamond-shaped design instead of the word "Black.") The player is betting on the eighteen black-colored numbers. If one of these numbers wins, the player is paid off at even money (1 to 1). The correct odds are 1⅑ to 1. The house's advantage is 5⁵⁄₁₉ percent.

Red-Color Bet: This is the same as a black-color bet except that the player places her chip(s) on the space marked "Red," or on the red diamond, and is betting on the eighteen red-colored numbers. If one of these numbers wins, the player is paid off at even money (1 to 1). The correct odds are 1⅑ to 1. The house's advantage is 5⁵⁄₁₉ percent.

Odd-Number Bet: The player places her chip(s) on the space of the layout marked "Odd." The player is betting on the eighteen odd numbers. If one of the odd numbers wins, the player is paid off at even money (1 to 1). The correct odds are 1⅑ to 1. The house's advantage is 5⁵⁄₁₉ percent.

Even-Number Bet: This is the same as the odd-number bet, except that the player is betting on the eighteen even numbers. If one of the numbers wins, the player is paid off at even money (1 to 1). The correct odds are 1⅑ to 1. The house's advantage is 5⁵⁄₁₉ percent.

Roulette is the casino game that has invited more systems "to break the bank" than all other casino games combined. So many systems have been created in an effort to beat the bank at Roulette by mathematicians and scientists that most casino operators, including Carl Cohen of the Sands, sometimes call it the "egghead's game." Professional male gamblers call it a "woman's game." Every now and then one of our national magazines unconsciously shills for the casinos when it runs an article describing some surefire system for winning at Roulette. The authors of these articles usually swear that the system was successfully used by a friend at Monte Carlo or Las Vegas, and promise the reader that if she is not greedy she can earn $100 to $200 a week playing the system. Probably the editor thought the writer of the article was an expert, when he was an "expert" in name only. However that may be, I do know that whenever an article touting a gambling system appears in a national magazine the gambling operators silently thank the author, editor, and publisher. I recently saw a young lady lose $6,000 at a Roulette table in the Sheraton Hotel Casino in Puerto Rico while playing a variation of the progressive, or double-up, system that had been described in a leading national magazine. I am sure she would never have lost so much if she had not believed implicitly that the system was workable. When I told her afterward that the only thing the system did was to help her lose her money faster, she replied that she had won several hundred dollars using the same system the night before, and wanted to know how I explained that. I said: "That's easy. You won simply because you had a streak of good luck. The system had nothing to do with it."

The most popular Roulette system used by women players is the D'Alembert System. It is based on what its proponents call the "Law of Equilibrium." This is nothing more than the doctrine of the Maturity of Chances, which mathematicians call the "Gambler's Fallacy." The theory is that any two opposite chances, such as red or black, odd or even, must sooner or later win an equal number of times. If red, for instance, dominates for a series of spins, it is only a question of time until black will make up its retard. The D'Alembert system player, therefore, after every losing bet, adds an additional chip or chips to her bet on the next spin, and after every winning bet reduces her bet by one or more chips. These players misinterpret the theory of probability. They think that these opposite chances will even up in a short run, whereas the probability theory gives only an approximate statement of what can be expected to happen in a very long run. The bank's favorable advantage of the 0 and 00 will, in the long run, break all players.

Thousands of women Roulette players refuse to believe this. Many of them haunt the casinos day after day, endlessly recording statistics, clocking how often certain numbers, colors, or combinations have or have not appeared in the last few hours, nights, and even weeks. No casino operator is ever worried that these players will come up with a workable system. In fact, on request, at the Caribe Hilton Casino the management will supply the addict with a chart on which the Roulette numbers are printed so that she can save time, paper, and pencil by merely checking off the winning numbers instead of having to write them down.

Some women compile all this data for a different reason. They compare their statistics with all sorts of probability calculations, hoping to find some indication that the wheel is biased. A wheel very seldom goes haywire of its own accord, and I can't think of any fault a wheel could develop by itself that would not be spotted by the management in very short order.

Several years ago a woman phoned me at my home in Fairview, New Jersey, from Dallas, Texas, with the exciting news that after ten years she had developed the perfect Roulette system. Mrs. Blank, as I shall call her, offered to let me in on this marvelous get-rich-quick system if I would deposit $15,000 to her credit in her Dallas bank, and added that if I was able to find a flaw in the system the money would be returned to me. If I failed to find a flaw in it, then she would keep the $15,000 and I could go to Las Vegas, use the system, and win it back in an evening of play.

When I pointed out that this proposition already had one flaw because the Las Vegas operators will not permit me to play at their gaming tables, she suggested that I could easily get some friend to play the system for me. I told her to read the chapter on systems in *Scarne on Dice,* which would tell her what I thought of systems in general. "I have," she replied, "but those were dice systems; mine is for Roulette."

She thought she had an answer for everything, and she ran up quite a phone bill before I could shake her, which I did by saying that I might be playing a convention date in Dallas shortly and that I would look her up when I got there.

I had forgotten all about this incident until years later a woman walked up to me in the Caribe Hilton Hotel Casino, where I was, and still am, gambling overseer. It was Mrs. Blank.

"My husband and I are spending our vacation here," she said.

"How is that perfect Roulette system of yours working?" I asked.

She replied: "My husband has been playing it here all week. He's won an average of $100 for each night's play. So, you see, Mr. Scarne, it does work."

"Shouldn't you warn your husband," I asked, "that I'm here? I might learn your system by watching him play."

She shook her head, and said, "We discovered that your casino manager knows it already."

"I saved myself the fifteen grand you wanted for it, didn't I?"

She laughed. "Yes, I guess it isn't worth quite so much as I thought then. But it still works."

At that moment a man walked up to her and said: "I just won another $110 at the Roulette table. We're $868 ahead of the game on eight nights' play."

Mrs. Blank introduced me to her husband, who proved to be a professor at a Texas college. I had seen him playing at the table, and I knew the system he was using. System gamblers at Monte Carlo and Nevada have used it for years, and it has appeared in several magazines under different names. Gamblers call it the "Cancellation System."

It consists of writing down a column of figures in serial order, beginning with 1. Suppose we use the sequence 1, 2, 3, 4, 5, 6,

7, 8, 9, 10. The player begins by betting the total of the top and bottom figures—in this instance, 11 chips. If she wins, she crosses out the top and bottom figures and then bets the total of the new top and bottom figures—in this instance, 9 plus 2, or 11. If the player loses, she adds the amount lost at the bottom of the column and then bets the total of the new top and bottom figures. In this instance she would bet 11 plus 2, or 13 chips. This procedure of betting and crossing out and adding numbers continues until all the numbers in the column have been crossed out.

As in most systems, the player must increase the amount of her bet after each loss. In the Cancellation System the player sticks to bets that pay even money, and the theory is that since she crosses out two numbers of her series when she wins and adds only one number when she loses, she must eventually cross out all numbers. When this happens, she will have won 55 betting units.

On paper it looks good, and I don't blame Mrs. Blank for first thinking she and her husband were on to a good thing. But, as she had already found out, there's no fortune in it. Her husband wasn't winning $15,000 in a night's play as she originally thought could be done; he was winning small amounts. What she found out later, after she and her husband lost $10,-000 on two successive plays, was that their $868 front money was won by being lucky and not by making use of a betting system.

The Cancellation System, like all other so-called systems, sooner or later is interrupted by the fact that the player goes broke. Since in this system the player increases her bets by small amounts, it takes her longer until her bets increase to the point where she is stopped by the house limit. But when a long losing streak hits the player, like the one that caused Mrs. Blank and her husband to lose $10,000, she finds herself so far in the hole that she has reached the limit of her own bankroll. Or she discovers that the constantly increasing size of her bets has put her in the position of having to risk a large amount of money to try to recoup her losses. At this point, afraid to risk a large-sized bet, she quits a loser, saying: "Well, it wasn't supposed to happen that way. I wonder what went wrong with the system."

Another catch is that if the table is busy, the croupier views the system player who places a long series of small bets with distaste. The player is giving him a lot of work, and he is very likely to make it clear that he doesn't want your business. "Look, lady," he'll say, "play your system somewhere else. We're busy now."

It doesn't matter what system you make use of, in the long run you can't overcome the house advantage of the single and double zero that the Roulette bank has stacked against you. This house advantage is the only surefire system that works as expected.

SCARNE'S ROULETTE SYSTEM FOR WOMEN

I have heard countless casino gamblers over the years, here and abroad, who have won tens of thousands of dollars at the game of Roulette, say, "You can't win at this game." You can, but if you are one of the many thousands of American women gamblers who dream of retiring on their future Roulette winnings, my advice to you is to stop dreaming, and banish the thought. I recommend that you play Roulette with a modest goal in mind. You may be lucky and win big over one or more sessions; but your chances of beating the wheel, if you play continuously through several long sessions, is very dubious.

To all women Roulette players I advise that you (1) Do not take the game seriously; (2) play Roulette for fun, not for profit; (3) budget yourself. Divide the amount of money you can afford to lose by the number of times you expect to play, and don't exceed that loss limit in any session. If you should find yourself ahead of the game by a good sum, pack the game in—tomorrow is another day.

The above advice, if followed, will make your Roulette-playing sessions more enjoyable, and you will never get hurt financially.

6

Slot Machines

The slot machine, or one-armed bandit, the Number One casino gambling pursuit of American women, was invented in 1895 by a twenty-nine-year-old San Francisco mechanic named Charles Fey. Today slot machines are found in gambling joints the world over—Europe, Latin America, Asia, Africa, and North America. The State of Nevada alone boasts of having over 20,000 slots. The nickel and quarter machines are the most popular in Nevada, and their action accounts for about 75 percent of the gamblers' yearly slot machine profits of some $60 million, of which $48 million is deposited by women slot players. The nickel and quarter slots are followed by the dime, half-dollar, silver-dollar, and one-cent machines, in that order.

What is the magnet that causes American women to contribute tens of millions of dollars yearly to the slot-machine industry? What is the fascination behind all this that causes most of these women constantly to keep feeding coins into one or more machines for hour after hour, receiving little or nothing in return? The reason is that most women are under the impression that slot machines are set to pay off jackpots after a certain amount of money has been fed into the slots and that the more coins they pour into the machine, the better are their chances of hitting the jackpot. They couldn't be more wrong.

Most gamblers believe that the operators can adjust a slot machine to pay out any percentage desired merely by turning some sort of screw inside the machine. This belief has arisen because a good many authors of books on games have written about slots without really knowing what the machines are like on the inside. The belief is not true. The mechanism of a slot machine is quite complicated, and the pay-back odds cannot be changed unless the wheel's symbols are repositioned and the pay and the payoff slots adjusted to coincide with the changed combinations on the wheel.

One-armed bandits are factory fixed to retain a certain percentage of the coins fed into them, which may run from a low 6 percent to a high of 50 percent or more. However, slots like Roulette or Craps pay off according to laws of probability. It's a waste of time and money to keep pouring money into a machine because of the belief that the more coins one pours into a machine, the closer the machine is to hitting the jackpot or big bonus. The chances of hitting the jackpot big bonus, or any other winning combination, is exactly the same with each spin of the wheels, and the amount of money previously fed into the machine can't alter this fact.

The modern, superdeluxe one-armed bandit, with its shiny chromium finish and its array of glowing neon lights, is a beautiful piece of machinery to behold, and a temptation very few women can resist.

Each slot machine is made up of some 300-odd parts, and is one of the few gambling devices with a mechanical banker that collects losing bets, pays off winning bets, and makes fewer mistakes than any human dealer in any banking game.

Every time a coin is fed into a three-wheel slot and the machine handle is pulled, three or four wheels are set rotating. The present-day three-wheel and four-wheel machines all have

20 symbols on each wheel, which may be cherries, plums, horse-shoes, melons, cowboys, oranges, lemons, stars, bells, bars, and so on. The wheels spin until a brake brings them to a stop, lining up various horizontal combinations of winning or losing symbols on the play line (center line) as seen through the small glass window atop each machine.

Basically, all the slot machines work the same way. You put a coin into the slot opening, pull the lever downward, and it spins the three or four wheels with the symbols. The lever pull also activates a small timer that permits the wheels to spin for a couple of seconds. Then a pawl rattles over the notches of each wheel and drops into one of them, stopping each wheel on a certain symbol as shown on the machine's pay line. The automatic payoffs on each machine are regulated by the manner in which the pawls come to rest on the notches of the wheels, forming paying or nonpaying combinations.

The number of possible combinations that can appear on the pay line of a three-wheel slot machine is 20 multiplied by 20 multiplied by 20, a total of 8,000. To get the number of possible combinations on a four-wheel slot machine, multiply once more by 20 for a total of 160,000.

But if you want to know your true chances of hitting the jackpot of one of the many standard three-wheel machines, let's study the bar symbols attached to the wheels of a standard one-armed bandit:

Symbols	1st Wheel	2nd Wheel	3rd Wheel
Cherries	5	7	3
Oranges	4	1	10
Plums	6	1	4
Bells	1	9	1
Horseshoes	2	1	1
Bars	2	1	1
	20	20	20

Out of the twenty symbols on the first wheel, two are bars, one on the second, and one on the third wheel, which makes your chances of winning a jackpot 1 in 4,000. Naturally, the jackpot combination isn't the only winning payoff; there are many others. Some modern slot machines are fixed to pay jackpots in many more ways than one; however, the machines are geared to retain the same percentage take. I repeat: The house's favorable slot-machine take in Nevada and Caribbean casinos runs from a low of 6 percent to a high of 50 percent or more. Most slots found in Las Vegas Strip casinos are geared to retain from 11 to 22 percent.

On one of my recent casino scouting missions in the Caribbean, I visited the now closed Lucayan Beach Hotel casino on Grand Bahama Island. I discovered that the sixty-odd "Bally" slot machines that lined the walls were engaged by women whose husbands or boyfriends, I later learned, were engaged in the art of shooting Craps or playing Blackjack. One of the women slot-machine players caught my attention, for she was guarding two machines and calling aloud for the slot attendant to get her $20 worth of quarters. When the attendant arrived with the change, the woman remarked: "The jackpots are due. I just missed the jackpot by one symbol on each of these two machines, and I'm not quitting until I hit both jackpots." She couldn't have been more wrong.

It's these near-hits that spur many women players on to lose more money at the machines than they can afford. Let me ask you this question: How often have you missed hitting the jackpot by one symbol, a symbol that came to a stop either above or below the pay line? Many times, no doubt. If it weren't for the fact that you can see a row of symbols above and below the machine's pay line, slot machines would lack their fascination, and would not be the big money-makers that they are. In brief, the little glass window that permits you to see the vertical row of symbols on the machine's pay line, or center line, also permits you to see a vertical row of like symbols above and below the pay line. Hence, through the machine's little window you will see 26 times more near-hits than actual hits. For example, let's suppose that you pulled the handle on a standard three-wheel machine 27 times, and each of these 27 times the three bars (jackpot symbols) were visible through the slot-machine window, and let's further suppose that they appeared in various combinations on the pay line, above or below the pay line exactly as predicted by probabilities. We would find that out of these 27 plays, the three bars would stop on the pay line on only one play. The remaining 26 plays would be near-hits. Bear in mind that I am discussing the proportion of near-hits to hits. That is, as I have shown, 26 to 1. But the proportion of misses (including complete misses as well as near-hits) is 4,000 to 1. So for this reason, Lady, don't let near-hits raise your blood pressure. The same holds true for all other winning combinations.

If you think that playing the slots is nothing more than a pleasant pastime, watch a few women slot addicts at work. I can name a dozen women players who have lost as much as $20,000 a year to the machines. For many addicts, putting coins into one machine isn't fast enough, so they tackle two, three, or four machines at the same time. The left hand puts a coin in; the right pulls the handle down with a practiced rhythmic motion; the player takes a sideward step, and repeats with the next machine, and the next and the next, then back to the first machine—hour after hour. Many women addicts wear a glove on the right hand to avoid getting calluses.

Here is an incident that—although it is a rare exception to jackpot payoffs—beautifully illustrates the fascination the machine holds for women in all walks of life. On the afternoon of August 6, 1958, five friends of mine—a socially prominent Chicago lady, her husband, and three friends—were walking through the casino at the Habana Hilton Hotel in Havana, Cuba, where I was gambling overseer for Conrad Hilton prior to Fidel Castro. The woman's husband found a nickel on the floor, handed it to his wife, and suggested she play it in one of the machines that line the walls. She dropped the coin in the nickel slot, pulled the lever, and found herself a five-coin winner.

Four hours later I came by and found the group glued to

the same machine. The woman, with a handful of nickels, was playing, and the four men were rooting for her to hit the jackpot. The husband, seeing me, said, "Scarne, this is all happening with a found nickel!"

I turned to his wife. "Why don't you play the nickel four-reel Buckaroo machine? You might hit the four buckaroos and collect the $125 bonus award."

"Let's go," she said, and a moment later was pulling madly at the Buckaroo lever, occasionally switching from right to left hand. After about fifteen minutes of average slot-machine payouts, Whammo! Four buckaroos on the pay line. The four friends let out a whoop that could be heard all over the casino, and play stopped momentarily at the Craps, Blackjack, Roulette, and Baccarat tables. A few minutes later, with the $125 award, my friend and her rooting section moved to a quarter Buckaroo machine. She played in about $10, and Lady Luck smiled again—a broad grin. She had hit the four buckaroos for the $625 prize award. More cheers rocked the casino.

After five hours of play, the group adjourned for dinner. After dinner she was back at the slots again. And she did little else for the next six days. She put in about 60 hours of slot play, during which she hit about 40 jackpots. After the first 40 hours, the found nickel had grown to $1,700. That would have been a good place to stop.

For the last two days of play she moved over to the silver-dollar machine, which awarded $2,500. An hour before leaving the hotel to catch a plane for home, she lost her last silver dollar. The found nickel was "lost" again; her hands were black from handling coins, and calloused as well. I told her that she had pulled the slot handle approximately 54,000 times.

She smiled, and said, "I enjoyed every one of those 54,000 pulls."

Of the thousands upon thousands of slot players I have seen here and in other countries, I can't recall one woman who ever ended by being a slot winner over an extended period of playing time. But I can easily recall the names of a dozen women who lost fortunes vainly trying to beat the slots.

At the Habana Hilton Casino I once overheard a woman slot player making the old, familiar complaint to my friend the casino host Allen Kanter.

"Mr. Kanter, I just dropped $20 in that quarter machine and got only four quarters back. Don't these slot machines ever pay off?"

Allen's reply was classic: "Lady, they sure do. They pay the casino's rent, the light bills, all the employees' salaries, and a cool half million dollars a year in net profits. Sure they pay off."

Because many illegal slot-machine operators here and abroad do not like to give the slot-machine player even one chance to hit the jackpot or the big bonus, they make use of a "bug." This is a small flat half-circle of iron, about an inch long, that looks something like a real bug. These crooks usually screw the bug on the inside of the machine's mechanism and close a cog that controls one of the three or four jackpot on bonus symbols, usually the one on the last wheel. When the wheels stop and the bugged symbol is about to appear on the pay line, the brake hits the bug and is prevented from slipping into the original opening of the cog. Hence this symbol must come to rest just above or below the pay line instead. The best you can get on a machine bugged this way is one symbol less than the jackpot or big bonus calls for.

If a jackpot or bonus symbol on the machine you are playing has a habit of slipping down or jumping up above the pay line after the wheels have come to a stop, it's one of two things: either the jackpot or bonus award is bugged or the machine isn't working properly. If you have been playing for hours, and have failed to see a jackpot or bonus symbol stop on the pay line of every one of the machine's wheels—it's a sure bet you're in a clip joint.

If this happens to you, don't complain to the management; just walk away quietly, because slot-machine crooks are dangerous people when caught red-handed.

Any woman who plays the one-armed bandits or those new-fangled coin-operated gambling devices for any purpose other than that of fun, dispelling boredom, or frittering away some expendable cash needs to have her head examined.

7

Bingo

Bingo, that great American gambling game, is the favorite weekly pastime of millions of American women living in cities, towns, and hamlets throughout the United States. My findings reveal that last year about 25 million Bingo players, of whom 23 million were women, played Bingo legally and illegally one or more times. Today, Bingo is played in most countries of Latin America, Europe, Africa, and Asia.

Bingo is really the old-fashioned Italian parlor game of Lotto, which is in turn derived from the more than 435-year-old Italian National Lottery. Although Bingo is actually a lottery in the true sense, and there is a charge for competing for prizes determined by chance, the game has been legalized in at least eleven states: New York, New Jersey, Nevada, Vermont, Connecticut, Rhode Island, New Hampshire, Minnesota, Maine, Maryland, and Alaska.

Bingo's great popularity is due primarily to two factors: The game is simple to play, and every game must produce one or more winners. Since a series of games is usually played in one

94

session, the game supplies hours of fun and tension. Only a game like Bingo could produce the phenomenon of a hall full of several hundred women who seldom make a sound except for cries of jubilation or disappointment at the end of each game.

This impressed an Englishman who visited this country back in 1940, and later told a friend at home: "American women play a very strange game. Can't recall its name, but it's played in a large hall by several hundred women seated at tables with a number of small cards before them. A man on an elevated platform constantly calls out numbers to which the women listen attentively, never saying a word, until suddenly one woman shouts at the top of her voice, 'Bingo!' and all the others exclaim, 'Aw, nuts!' " Bingo playing is legal in England, and now is almost as popular there as it is in this country.

I can't see why some reformers call Bingo a "growing national problem." None of the players loses a great sum. At an average cost of $4 per session (actually, only $2 over the long run, because half of the money wagered is returned in prizes), millions of women, mostly middle-aged and elderly ladies who have few, if any, outlets for their gambling urge, buy hours of sociability, excitement, and fun playing a game that also provides considerable sums for worthy causes and community projects.

As it is played today, Bingo is a form of lottery because the game calls for the sale and distribution of printed cards. However, unlike lotteries, Bingo cards cannot be purchased outside the Bingo premises; each player must be present to cover the drawn numbers on her Bingo card with markers while the actual game is taking place.

Modern Bingo equipment is composed of Bingo cards, made of either cardboard or paper, with a playing surface that bears a printed design of 5 rows of 5 squares each—25 squares in all. The letters B-I-N-G-O appear above this design, each letter above one of the vertical columns. All the squares contain numbers except the center square, which is considered a free play. The following arrangement of numbers is standard, and appears on most Bingo cards:

The first vertical row on the left under the letter *B* contains any five numbers from the group 1 through 15. Under *I* there are any five numbers from the group 16 through 30. Under *N*, the center vertical row, there are only four numbers from the group 31 through 45. The middle square of this row is the center square of the card, and it is either blank or bears a printed *O* or *X* or the words *Free Play*. Under *G* in the fourth vertical row are any five numbers from the group 46 through 60, and under *O* in the fifth row any five numbers from the group 61 through 75.

In many Bingo parlors one, two, or three Bingo cards are pasted on a larger heavy cardboard called a "lapboard." This prevents the players from taking the cards home as souvenirs, and the board serves as a table.

The latest Bingo innovation is the fingertip Bingo card, which requires no markers. Slides can be moved to cover each of the card's 25 squares.

The most popular device for selecting numbers is the Bingo bowl, often called the Bingo cage, a spherical wire-mesh cage, about 9½ inches in diameter, into which the Bingo balls are placed. It is mounted on a wooden or metal base, and has a crank-turning, ball-selecting device. There are 75 bingo balls, each of which bears one of the letters of the word "Bingo" and a number. The letter-*B* balls bear numbers from the 1 through 15 group; the letter *I* balls bear numbers from the 16 through 30 group; and so on—the same grouping arrangement as on the cards.

When the operator turns the crank, the wire cage revolves and the players can see the balls being mixed. When he stops turning the crank, an opening at the bottom of the cage releases one ball.

Another popular device for mixing and selecting the balls is the Bingo blower, which consists of a glass enclosure into which 75 lettered and numbered Ping-Pong balls are placed. An electric air compressor sends a stream of air into the glass case, agitating and mixing the balls until one ball falls into a small pocket and then drops out of the enclosure.

An announcer, known as the caller, calls the letter and number of the released ball over a loudspeaker. If, for example, *B*5 is drawn, players whose cards bear a 5 in the *B* column place a cardboard or plastic marker over it. This is called "covering the number." The caller then places the drawn ball on a master board, which is often connected to an electrically operated panel that lights up the number on a large flashboard so that it can be seen as well as heard. The master board is also used as a check on the drawn numbers.

As soon as any player succeeds in covering five numbers in a straight line on her card, vertically, horizontally, or diagonally, she shouts, "Bingo!" A floorman or floorwoman goes to the player and reads the covered numbers on the player's card aloud to the caller or a tallyman for verification. If the caller confirms that these five numbers have been drawn, the player is declared the winner of the game and the prize.

In many Bingo parlors the jackpot game is a two-way play. Some parlors have added three- and four-way plays, although the jackpot is the important factor. The player who first covers a straight-line combination wins a prize, but the big prize, or jackpot, goes to the player who first covers her entire board. This is called a coverall, or blackout.

If two or more players get a winning position at the same time, the prize money is divided equally.

Many Bingo parlors also feature a four-way play, or round robin in which there are four winning positions:

1. The covering of five numbers in a straight line in any direction.
2. The covering of the four numbers at the four corners of the card.
3. The covering of the eight numbers that surround the center "freeplay" square.
4. The covering of all the numbers on the card.

Some Bingo parlors consider as winning plays the covering of two or three straight lines when they cross or intersect so as to form the letters *X,U,L,H,* or *T.* Some parlors give a double bonus for specific straight-line positions of five numbers, such as the top line, the bottom line, and so on.

Recently some Bingo operators have added an extra ball that is distinctively colored and bears no letter or number. It acts as a wild number. In some games, when this ball is drawn, a player can cover any number on her card at any time during the game; sometimes it can be used only to cover the last number completing the winning position.

At the end of each game, after the awarding of the prize or prizes, all players clear their card or cards of markers and either retain them or exchange them for the next game. They may also purchase additional cards.

Bingo operators have also created a number of special features to stimulate business, such as early-bird tickets, which are sold at a special discount to induce players to come to the parlor early. Sometimes intermission tickets are also sold at a discount in the hope of continuing the Bingo action throughout the intermission period. There are also junior-jackpot tickets that pay off a smaller jackpot. Actually, all these specials have the same purpose: to relieve the Bingo player of more cash.

The admission ticket to a Bingo parlor usually costs $1, and the player gets one card called an "all-night board." Additional single-game cards usually cost 25 cents each. Most women play more than one card at a time, and it is not uncommon to see a woman playing as many as twenty-one cards at once, a total cost to her of $6. If you think that playing twenty-one cards simultaneously is a relaxing way to spend an evening, just try it. I have, and you can't relax for a second. It's hard work. But the women love it.

Many Bingo parlors in states where Bingo is not legal have a special jackpot that must be won in a specified number of drawn balls. For example, a jackpot coverall winner must be declared within the first fifty numbers drawn. If there should be no winner at one session, an additional $200 or more is added to the jackpot the following week. Jackpots of this kind, starting with $500, have been known to reach $10,000 and more before being won.

After clocking a great many Bingo players in different parts of the country, I found that at Bingo halls in New York and New Jersey, where the limit jackpot payoff is $250, the average player spends $4 per session. Some women spend as much as $7 per session; very few spend as little as the $1 admission fee. Mrs. Millie Stueben, an avid Bingo player from my neck of the woods, summed it up this way: "A person would look awfully cheap sitting through several hours of Bingo playing with just the one admission card."

The Bingo player will be interested to learn that her chances of hitting the coverall jackpot in 55 or less drawn numbers is approximately 1 in 10,000. In a hall crowded with several hundred women, where the complete set of 3,000 Bingo cards is in use, the chances of someone hitting the jackpot coverall in 55 or less drawn numbers is approximately 1 in 3 (3,000 in 10,000).

Here, in tabular form, are the chances a one-card holder has of making a coverall in 50, 51, 52, 53, 54, or 55 drawn numbers:

Total Numbers Drawn	Chances of Making a Coverall with One Card
50 or less	1 in 212,085
51 or less	1 in 112,284
52 or less	1 in 60,458
53 or less	1 in 33,081
54 or less	1 in 18,379
55 or less	1 in 10,359

Most women Bingoists that I scouted during my survey take from six to ten cards at a time because this increases the odds in their favor. It does, if the price of the extra cards is less than the price of the original admission card. If the price of the original card is $1, and the price of extra cards is 25 cents, here's how it breaks down. Let's say there are 300 original admission cards at $1 each, of which you have one. Your chances of winning the Bingo prize is 299 to 1. If you buy 4 extra cards at 25 cents each, you have 5 chances in 204. This is obviously better than 1 in 299; but you paid a total of $2, twice as much as your neighbor who has only one card. Therefore, to get your odds to the equivalent of your neighbor's, divide by 2. For your dollar you have 2½ chances in 203 to your neighbor's 1 in 203. However, if the price of the extra cards is the same as that for the original card, you may get more excitement with the extra card, but no better odds. Since the total prize awards for each game remain the same, whether 300 or 500 cards are sold, it is the Bingo operator who really profits when extra cards are sold.

When run by charitable organizations, Bingo is relatively free of the crookedness that accompanies many other forms of gambling. A few professional operators who run Bingo games at fairgrounds, amusement centers, and other public places are not always satisfied with their percentage take, and cheat the players of the big jackpot prizes they have advertised.

It's a simple dodge. They plant a house player, usually a woman, in the crowd who wins the big prize and later returns it, receiving only a fee for her day's or night's work. She wins because she is given a couple of Bingo boards whose numbers have been recorded on a sheet of paper that the announcer keeps within view. Sometimes identifying marks are placed near the numbers on the master board that correspond with those on the house player's cards. Then, as he draws the balls from the cage, the announcer miscalls one or more numbers. If, for example, he sees that the house player needs B8 and G47 to go Bingo, he pretends to read these two numbers from the next two balls drawn. The house player shouts "Bingo!" The announcer goes through the motions of confirming the numbers as the usher checks the player's card; then the announcer nonchalantly replaces the miscalled balls in the Bingo cage. The plant collects the jackpot, and the other players are none the wiser.

Another method employed by cheating Bingo announcers to steal the jackpot is accomplished as follows: The announcer's woman plant takes a front seat as close as possible to the announcer, making sure that no other player will be between them. To help facilitate the scheme, the woman plant plays ten or more Bingo cards. The announcer continues drawing and calling numbers until his plant cues him by lifting and turning her head toward him. This is the signal that informs the announcer that the plant requires one number to hit the jackpot. Once contact is made between the announcer and plant, the plant inaudibly calls the desired number. This is strictly a lip expression. The announcer, accustomed to the plant's lip movements, gets the message, and miscalls the next drawn number by calling the signaled number. The plant then shouts, "Bingo!" and the suckers are left holding the bag.

Bingo players can protect themselves from the above described methods of cheating by selecting one player to sit beside the announcer and check the numbers on the balls as they are drawn. A random choice of a player could easily be made by having the announcer, with his back to the audience, throw out a Ping-Pong ball, the person catching it being the one to act as checker. This checking would be necessary only when the Big Special or Big Jackpot is being played. If you suggest this procedure to your Bingo operator, and he welcomes your recommendation, he's honest. If he doesn't, then you would be wise to find yourself another Bingo parlor.

8

Keno—Nevada Style

Visit any Keno parlor in Nevada, and you will find that on the average three out of five players are women. This great popularity among women gamblers is due primarily to two factors: The game is played somewhat like the very well-known and very popular Bingo; and then there are the continuous casino advertisements of the $25,000 Keno jackpots that build fascinating dreams of hitting the $25,000 gigantic jackpot. All one has to do to win one of these $25,000 Keno jackpots is to plunk down a couple of bucks and pick from 8 to 15 lucky numbers out of a total of 20 numbers selected at random out of 80.

In all the years I have visited Nevada, I have heard of only one person collecting a $25,000 Keno jackpot—which event was followed by a casino investigation that resulted in the firing of a number of Keno clerks.

As played in Nevada casinos, Keno differs from regular Keno in several ways. Standard Keno, like Bingo, requires large numbers of players for successful operation of the game; the purchase price of a Keno or Bingo ticket is the same for all players, and these game sessions lasting only a few hours are usually run once a week.

Keno, Nevada style, on the other hand, can be dealt to one or more players; each player selects from 1 to 15 numbers, and can wager any amount she likes on her selection, providing it is within the house maximum betting limit. Keno parlors in Nevada operate twenty-four hours a day, with a new game being dealt every few minutes.

Most Nevada parlors seat twenty or more players. They contain several tables loaded with Keno tickets, and the players are supplied with either black crayons or ink and brushes. Each ticket bears the numbers 1 to 80, and on her ticket the player marks the number or numbers she wishes to play. A great number of different bets can be made at Keno because the players can select various combinations of numbers. A 1-Spot Ticket is one on which a player has marked, and is betting on, a single number. If that number appears in the 20 drawn numbers, the player wins. When she marks two numbers, it is a 2-Spot Ticket, and she wins if both numbers appear among the 20 that are drawn. She may mark and bet on groups of as many as 15 numbers. That is known as a 15-Spot Ticket, but the most popular ticket is the 10-Spot Ticket.

The play of the game is as follows: Once the player has marked her ticket, she presents her cash (which usually averages from $1 to $5) and the marked ticket at the Keno counter, where the clerk makes two duplicates by punching out the player's numbers on a house ticket, adds the amount wagered and the number of the game to be next played. The clerk gives the player one copy, and retains the original and the other copy.

When it is time for the drawing to begin, an announcement is made over the loudspeaker, and everyone gathers to watch. The Keno blower, which is elevated behind the Keno counter, contains 80 Ping-Pong balls numbered 1 through 80. The operator starts the Keno blower, and the Ping-Pong balls can be seen as they are being thoroughly mixed by a constant stream of compressed air. Then, one by one, they are drawn. As each ball is drawn, its number is called and flashed on the electrically lighted Keno boards for the players to check against their tickets. When the twentieth ball has been drawn, the game ends. With bated breath each player compares her ticket with the drawn numbers, and the winners go to the Keno counter to collect. Minutes later, a new game is played.

Keno Instructions

1-SPOT TICKET .... $1–$2–$5–$10
Catch 1 Number .... Pays $3.20 for $1

2-SPOT TICKET
Catch 2 Numbers .... Pays 13 for 1

3-SPOT TICKET
Catch 2 Numbers .... Money Back
Catch 3 Numbers .... Pays 47 for 1

4-SPOT TICKET
Catch 2 Numbers .... Money Back
Catch 3 Numbers .... Pays 47 for 1
Catch 4 Numbers .... Pays 118 for 1

5-SPOT TICKET
Catch 3 Numbers .... Pays 3 for 1
Catch 4 Numbers .... Pays 26 for 1
Catch 5 Numbers .... Pays 332 for 1

The 1-Spot Ticket is the simplest form of Keno betting. If you select one number and wager $1 and win, you receive $3.20 ($2.20 plus your $1), which means the odds you received were 2.2 to 1. What most women Keno players don't stop to consider is that although only 1 number out of 20 has to be picked, those 20 are selected at random out of 80. In other words, there are 80 numbers on your ticket, and 20 of the numbers are drawn— so your chance of winning is 20 in 80, or 1 out of 4. So it costs

$4 to win $3.20; the house take on 4 $1 bets on a 1-Spot Ticket is 80 cents, or 20 percent. This makes the 1-Spot Ticket one of the biggest sucker bets in the casino.

If you play a 2-Spot Ticket for $1 and win, you receive $13, when the correct payoff should be about $16.60—this time the house bite is 21.8 percent. This makes the 2-Spot Ticket a worse bet than the 1-Spot Ticket. The 3-Spot, 4-Spot, 5-Spot, 6-Spot, 8-Spot, 9-Spot, 10-Spot, 11-Spot, 12-Spot, 13-Spot, 14-Spot, and 15-Spot tickets, as well as similar tickets such as 12-Spot High-Low Ticket, 10-Spot Group of 5, Deuce Ways Group of 2, 9-Spot Groups of 3, and others, average about 23 percent against the player.

Of the millions of dollars wagered by women at Keno, about 60 percent is bet on the 10-Spot Ticket. A $2.50 bet on a 10-Spot Ticket can net you a $25,000 jackpot:

10-SPOT TICKET

Catch 5 Numbers	Pays 2 for 1
Catch 6 Numbers	Pays 18 for 1
Catch 7 Numbers	Pays 180 for 1
Catch 8 Numbers	Pays 1,300 for 1
Catch 9 Numbers	Pays 2,600 for 1
Catch 10 Numbers	Pays 10,000 for 1

What are your chances of betting $2.50 on a 10-Spot Ticket and hitting the $25,000 jackpot? Your chance of accomplishing this feat is about 1 in 9 million. Yet, daily, hundreds of women Keno players are hoping to achieve this miracle. But there are other winning payoffs that are not quite so improbable. Picking 9 numbers will bring a payoff of 2,600 for 1; here the chance is about 1 in 163,000. Picking 8 numbers pays off at odds of 1,300 for 1; here the chance is about 7,000 to 1. And so on down the line, to picking 5 numbers, which pays off at even money, with about 1 chance in 20 of happening. If 4 or fewer numbers are picked there is no payoff.

However, because each casino has a $25,000 maximum payoff limit on each game to aggregate players, and if two outstandingly lucky players were to hit the $25,000 giant jackpot, they would have to share the remains of the $25,000 jackpot after the smaller winners were paid.

A final bit of advice to women Keno players: Don't gamble your money away expecting to win a $25,000 Keno jackpot, because this is 29 times more difficult than winning the Irish Hospitals' Sweepstakes top prize of $140,000.

9

The Numbers Game

The most popular illegal form of lottery betting in the United States today is the Numbers game. Sample findings of my survey reveal that about 16,000,000 American women played the numbers one or more times during 1966. My sample findings further indicate that 1 out of 2 colored females living in big cities play the numbers regularly.

A conservative estimate of the 1966 women's Numbers game betting handle in the United States was a gigantic $3 billion. This $3 billion Numbers handle for 1966 was greater than the total handle of all combined lotteries and raffles in this country, which includes Bingo and Keno, as well as the privately operated Irish Hospitals' Sweepstakes.

Why so many women go for the numbers is characteristically evident in the experiences of Mary, a barmaid in Newark, New Jersey. Everybody in the neighborhood is talking about Mary. The other day Mary hit 317 for $10 for a take of $5,000—which she used as a down payment on a new home. Mary's friends—including Mary herself—think she was mighty lucky. I don't.

Mary could have bought a new home a long time ago if she had saved the $20 a day she and her husband have been betting on the numbers for the past several years. Mary and her friends have forgotten that she gambled away many times $5,000 before her lucky hit. Lady, that's something to remember the next time you hear of a big winner in the Numbers game.

My own sample findings of what makes the Numbers game so attractive to women show that: (*a*) Women are natural suckers for big odds—the 500-for-1 Numbers odds are tempting to most women; (*b*) women Numbers players can select their own numbers and bet their money on their favorite lucky numbers. And what woman doesn't have at least one lucky number. (*c*) You can make small bets: 25 cents, 50 cents, and sometimes even pennies. In addition, the action is daily, and the players get the Numbers result the same night from the racing section of most metropolitan newspapers. All of these factors combined make them feel that the Numbers game is honest.

Playing the numbers was once referred to as a poor person's way of expressing his or her gambling instinct, since its participants used to bet pennies on the illusive three digits. Things are different today. Of the 16 million women who play the numbers, it is doubtful if one out of a hundred wagers less than 25 cents on a number. The daily average bet on the numbers for women living in metropolitan areas of the United States ranges from $1 to $2. Many women, however, bet $10 to $20 or more on a single three-digit number, and a few women highrollers think nothing of betting $100 or more on a "hot number," especially one they dreamed of the night before.

Most women today wouldn't bet money on a fortuneteller's prediction based on a layout of cards or tea leaves, or on the juggling of some astrological figures. But most women numbers players believe that the sight or mention of any three-digit number is a psychic sign and that some supernatural force has brought it to their attention. Millions of dollars are bet by women numbers players every day on what they consider is their lucky number for the day: their street address, the last three digits of their birth year, the sales total of a purchase, the license number of a passing car.

The favorite reading matter of millions of women players is (*a*) the newspapers that report the winning numbers; and (*b*) dream books and numerology pamphlets that give interpretations of dreams, daily happenings, birthdays, and so on, in terms of three-digit numbers. *Know Your Dream, Lucky Star, King Tut,* and *Gypsy Queen* are among the best sellers in New York City.

The system is simple: If you dreamed last night that you took a trip on a bus, look under Travel. You are told that "traveling means you will change jobs (213)." If you dreamed of visiting a lawyer, this means "you will suffer from a cold (165)." Dreaming of money: "Your luck will change (381)"; dancing girls denote "happiness, and you will come into money (814)." A doctor denotes pregnancy (119) for a woman and illness for a man (415). Oddly enough, although many of these books are published by the same company, they all give different interpretations and numbers.

Here's a Numbers-game incident that happened right under my nose not so long ago. I was having breakfast with my lifelong friend Jack Reme in Jack's Diner in Fairview, New Jersey, when a woman patron whom we'll call Jane sat down at the counter and began telling about a dream she had had the night before. Dramatically, she emphasized the fact that one of the most important features of the dream was a vivid impression in bright lights of the number 614.

"In my dream," she went on, "I gave Gimp [the neighborhood runner] two bucks to bet on 614 and I remember seeing a lot of other people betting on the same number. Gimp picked up $30 worth of bets, and 614 won. Gimp brought in a grip full of money, and paid everybody off." There was only one thing to do about a dream as definite as all that, and Jane did it. She phoned Gimp, who made his headquarters at Abe's newsstand across the street. He came to the diner. Jane gave him a $2 bet on Number 614, and other patrons of the diner began betting quarters, halves, and dollars on 614. Within an hour Gimp had collected $30 worth of action. The betting stopped at that point because the bettors figured that if they exceeded the amount in Jane's dream they might put the hex, or evil eye, on the number.

Believe it or not, that afternoon the winning mutuel number at Belmont was 614. All the bettors were happy, and those who hadn't believed in dreams before were converted.

The next morning Gimp arrived at the diner to pay off. The payoff price at that time was 600 to 1, and runners did not collect the 10 percent commission on winning numbers. A bettor who wagered $2 received $1,200, a 50-cent bet collected $300, and a ten-cent bet got $60. It was a big day at Jack's Diner. Gimp paid off a total of $16,800. Another $1,200 should have been paid to Jane, but she didn't come in all day. Was she ill? If so, it must be something really serious: Jane would have left her own funeral to collect that $1,200.

A friend of Jane's told me later that she had gone to visit friends in Chicago, but I got the straight story from Gimp shortly afterward.

"John," he said, "you'll never believe this one. I wasn't getting any business out of Jack's Diner, so I got Jane to shill for me with her dream story. The 614 number I just picked out of the air. If my boss, the head runner, knew I touted all these people on 614, I'd be out of a job."

"And just where," I asked, "is the missing Jane?"

"Scarne, she's really sick. She's at home, but she's staying under cover. She owes a lot of money to people around town, and they expect to get paid because they heard about the $1,200 she won on the number she dreamed."

"So why doesn't she pay off from her winnings?"

"That's why she's sick. She didn't bet a penny on 614. I gave her that $2 to bet to make it look good. And I didn't put that bet into my book. It makes me sick, too."

This story leaked after a while, and Jane left town. One memory of Fairview I'm sure she'll always have is Number 614.

Let's take a good look at the Numbers game. Although it's illegal in every state, city, or hamlet, if you know your way around it won't be difficult to find a numbers runner who'll accept your bet.

The winning number is usually based upon the last digits—three in all—of the daily mutuel betting handle at a major metropolitan racetrack. Let's say that Monday's mutuel betting handle for nine races at New York's Aqueduct Racetrack was $2,586,123. Monday's winning number is 123. If, on the other hand, you were lucky enough to have bet $1 on that number, you are a winner; and since such a bet pays off at odds of 500 for 1, you receive $500 in return. Some banks, however, pay off at 450-to-1 odds, others at 600-for-1 odds.

Another bet permitted at the Numbers game is known as "boxing." When you write your number on the betting slip, you may box it by drawing a square around it. This indicates that you are betting on all possible combinations of the chosen number, and it is known as a six-way combination bet. If you select number 125 and box it, you are betting on 125, 152, 215, 251, 512, and 521. Of course, this reduces the payoff to one-sixth. If the bank pays 500 for 1 on a straight bet a six-way payoff should be 83⅓ for 1; but the operators round the number to 80, and the payoff is 80 for 1.

Any straight or head number that contains two identical digits (such as 121, 323, 556) is known as a three-way combination because only three different combinations can be made with it. If you box Number 121, for instance, you are betting on 121, 112, and 211. Since most banks pay only 80 for 1, the same as on a six-way combination, it is sheer lunacy to box numbers of this sort.

Most banks insist that the player also bet on a straight number with each combination or box-number bet.

What chance does that lucky number of yours have of hitting and paying off? No complicated mathematics is needed to figure this answer. There are 1,000 numbers from 000 to 999, and one of them wins. You have 1 chance in 1,000, which means that the odds are 999 to 1 against you. Every player has an equal chance, and the odds remain the same for any number selection, even if it is a repeat of yesterday's winning number or one that hasn't appeared in years.

Most banks pay off at less than the usual odds on "cut and disaster numbers." These are numbers that get too much play because too many players believe they are lucky numbers. Some banks issue a cut-number sheet listing nearly 200 cut numbers. In some sections of New Jersey any three-number digit whose middle number is a 1, such as 010, 015, 116, 217, and so on, is a cut number and is paid off at 400-for-1 odds. Should a newspaper carry a three-digit number on its front page showing a cracked-up automobile whose license plate reads XY151—the number 151 is a catastrophe number as far as the numbers operators are concerned and winners get paid off at odds of 400 for 1.

The Numbers-game operators give various reasons as to why they cut as many as 200 numbers, but true or false, cutting numbers reduces the players' winnings considerably.

If the correct odds on hitting three numbers are 999 to 1 and the bank pays only 500 for 1, and in the case of cut numbers 400 for 1, it should be obvious by now that the only people who consistently make a profit at the Numbers game are the operators, their employees, and the politicians and cops who sell protection.

There's not much point in advising a Numbers player to forget about her favorite game, and gamble, if she must, at some game whose unfavorable percentage isn't so high. The many women players I know just don't listen to such advice. If you want to play because it's fun, and are willing to pay the price, that's your business, but if you play because you figure to come out ahead, baby, you can forget it. If you have read this far, you'll know that bucking a house edge of from 50 to 60 percent is a sure way to a pauper's grave.

Want proof? O.K. Suppose you should decide to gamble exactly $1,000 on the numbers in one week. You decide to bet an equal amount on each of the 1,000 possible numbers. Your bank pays off at 500-for-1 odds. On Monday you bet $1 on each of the 1,000 numbers, and you know for sure one of them will win. The last three digits of the total day's handle at the Belmont track turns out to be 225, and your runner pays you $500.

Since your $1,000 bankroll has already shrunk to $500, the most you can bet on each number Tuesday is 50 cents. You win again, and collect $250. Your loss for two days' play is $750. You should realize by now that you are on a one-way street and headed for the cleaners. On Wednesday you bet $250 on the 1,000 numbers, 25 cents on each. This time the winning number pays you $125. On Thursday you bet $120, 12 cents on each number, and pocket the remaining $5. The winning number pays you $60. On Friday you bet $60 by putting 6 cents on each number. You're lucky again—if that's what you want to call it—and your runner pays off with a smile—a big $30. You now take inventory, but it isn't likely that you are smiling. You have winnings of $30 plus the $5 you pocketed for a total of $35. You stick with the plan and bet $30 on Saturday with a 3-cent bet on each of the 1,000 numbers. You win $15, add it to the $5 you pocketed, for a total of $20. Subtract this from the $1,000 you started with, and the price you have paid for a week's fling at the exciting game of Numbers is $980.

Is the game all that exciting? Do you still think you can beat the Numbers and come out ahead?

10

Lotteries

THE IRISH HOSPITALS' SWEEPSTAKES

Of all the illegal lotteries for which tickets are sold in this country, the most heralded and widely played is that of the Irish Hospitals' Sweepstakes. Millions of Irish Hospitals' Sweepstakes tickets, priced at $2.80 each, are purchased by women in this country each year. The winning cash prizes range from a low consolation prize of $56 to a high grand prize of $140,000 —based upon a drawing and the results of a British horse race.

Contrary to the views held by most Americans, the Irish Hospitals' Sweepstakes is not operated by the Irish Free State Government. It is run by a privately owned company, known as the Hospitals' Trust, Ltd., of Dublin, Ireland. In 1930 the Irish Dail, or Parliament, passed an act permitting the Hospitals' Trust, Ltd., to run such a sweepstakes for the benefit of Irish hospitals.

Most of the women purchasers of Sweepstakes tickets that I have spoken to have no idea how the winners are determined, and don't understand why two or more persons living in a large metropolitan area win the $140,000 and the $56,000 top

114

prizes year in and year out. As I see it, the great popularity of the Irish Hospitals' Sweepstakes is due to the system of having dozens of groups of winners by dividing the total prize money into 120,000-pound units. At the present rate of exchange of about $2.80 to the pound, this is a payoff total of $336,000 for each unit group of winners. After the total amount of money available for prizes is divided into 120,000-pound units, any remaining sum is divided into fifty cash prizes of equal amounts for each group. Here is how each 120,000-pound ($336,000) unit is divided into prizes:

Holder of Winning Horse receives	$140,000
Holder of Second Horse receives	56,000
Holder of Third Horse receives	28,000
Drawers of Unplaced Horses share	84,000
70 Consolation Prizes of $280 each	19,600
150 Consolation Prizes of $56 each	8,400
TOTAL PRIZES	$336,000

Example: Let's assume that the money for prize awards totaled $10,180,000; by dividing this total by $336,000 (group of winners) we get 30 groups of winners, plus $100,000, which is divided into 50 residual prizes of $2,000 each. In other words, 30 persons will each receive a grand prize of $140,000; 30 persons will each receive a second prize of $56,000; and so on.

This procedure has changed the Irish Hospitals' Sweepstakes into a true lottery because the value of the prize awards is fixed and known in advance to the ticket purchaser. In the usual sweepstakes the value of the awards is not known in advance because it is determined by the sum of money in the pool when it closes.

How the winners are determined: There are three Irish Sweepstakes drawings each year, coupled with the running of the famous English horse races: the Grand National Steeplechase, the Epsom Downs Derby, and the Cambridgeshire Stakes. After you buy a ticket and have received an official receipt, your chances of winning are as good as those of any other ticket buyer. Your stub, bearing your name (or nom de plume) and address, is held with millions of others under lock and key at the Dublin headquarters. About ten days before the running of the determining race, a government watchdog committee, headed by the superintendent of the Garda Siochana (Irish Police), places the tickets in a number of huge pneumatic machines that shuffle and reshuffle them with blasts of compressed air for three days.

On the day of the drawing the tickets are placed in a giant drum that has forty-eight portholes giving access to its interior. Nurses of those hospitals that are the Sweeps beneficiaries take their places at the drum before an assembly of government officials and members of the press who represent numerous papers all over the world. As the great drum revolves, a nurse reaches through one of the portholes and draws out a ticket stub. Simultaneously, another nurse draws from a nearby smaller drum the printed names of the horses entered in the race. The number of the stub and the name of the horse are announced, recorded by auditors of the watchdog committee, and microfilmed to prevent any error or switching. For example: Stub No. R.P.V. 26115 is drawn from the giant drum at the same time that the name of the horse Fairy Stone is drawn from the small drum. The owner of the ticket whose name is on the stub thus has Fairy Stone as his horse in the race to be run the following week. The printed name of each horse harbored in the smaller drum is duplicated once for each $336,000 prize unit to be paid to winners.

This procedure is repeated until the names of the horses in the small drum have all been drawn. Then more stubs are drawn from the large drum to determine the winners of the smaller consolation prizes.

The following week the scheduled race to determine the top prize winners is run, and another running of the Irish Hospitals' Sweepstakes has come to pass. Winners are immediately notified by cable of their good fortune.

How many Sweepstakes tickets are sold annually throughout the United States? What are your chances of drawing a horse that wins? These are questions that no one in the Sweeps organization will answer. A study of the Sweepstakes operation, plus some deduction and calculation, has suggested to me the following answers, which I believe are very close to the correct ones:

Your Chances of Hitting the Irish Hospitals' Sweepstakes

1 chance in 305,000 of drawing the winning horse

1 chance in 101,666 of drawing a horse that places 1st, 2nd, or 3rd

1 chance in 3,470 of drawing a horse listed as a possible starter

1 chance in 1,000 of winning a prize of any size from $56 to $140,000

Although you have only 1 chance in 305,000 of winning a top prize of $140,000, your chance of winning a prize award of some sort is 1 in 1,000, which is exactly the same as the 1 in 1,000 chance the policy-numbers player has of hitting his three-digit number.

Although the entire Sweepstakes operation is illegal in this country, the Internal Revenue Bureau and state tax collectors aren't a bit hesitant about taking a big bite out of any prize money you win. If the head of a family of four whose annual income is $7,500 wins one of the top Sweeps prizes of $140,000, Uncle Sam's cut is about $63,000, leaving the winner a net of about $77,000. In New York City the state takes another $13,700 in income tax and New York City takes $2,660, leaving the lucky winner with about $60,640, or less than one-third of his prize.

A few winners have tried keeping their good fortune secret, hoping to avoid the tax by not reporting it; but the Internal Revenue boys notify them of their tax burden before they receive the cash. There is one legal gimmick by which a Sweeps purchaser can reduce the tax bite: he can divide the ownership of the ticket by signing more than one name on the ticket stub. If the head of a family of four who won $140,000 had listed three co-owners, each would be entitled to 25 percent, or $35,000. Filing four separate returns would cut the total $63,000 tax down to about $50,200, a saving of $12,800. This is legal, provided the partnership is in good faith and not just a tax-evasion scheme.

Many winners have gone to Dublin to collect, mistakenly believing that this would avoid the United States tax bite. Some have even established themselves as bona fide residents of Ireland, only to discover later that the Internal Revenue Bureau takes the position that the prize money was won while they were living in the States, and that later foreign residence of whatever duration does not exempt them from taxes. Uncle Sam has a good memory and a lot of patience, and a winner who doesn't return for years will still find a Treasury man waiting to greet him.

PUERTO RICO'S LOTTERY

Prior to 1964, the only legal lottery under the American flag was the government-sponsored lottery of Puerto Rico. The Puerto Rican lottery, like most of those in Latin America, has a weekly drawing. The top prize, El Primero, is $100,000. Twice a year, near Christmas and the Fourth of July, there are big drawings in which El Primero is $400,000, and is called El Gordo (The Fat One). The lottery prize money is all tax free.

Only 50,000 tickets are sold each week, many of which are illegally purchased by Puerto Ricans living in the New York area. Each ticket has eighty "pieces," or parts, worth 25 cents each for a total of $20 per ticket. Buyers may purchase as many pieces of as many tickets, or the entire ticket of one number, or as many tickets, as they desire. The miscellaneous prize numbers are determined by number approximation, sequence, and relation of ending numbers to the first-prize number. There are 7,905 prizes drawn each week, ranging from a low of $20 to a high of $100,000. The purchase of $1/80$th of a ticket in the regular weekly drawing costs 25 cents and the winner collects $1,250. A $1/80$th piece of a top winning ticket in one of the two special drawings costs $1 and pays off $5,000.

The weekly drawing takes place in the Lotería building in San Juan, the capital of Puerto Rico, and is made with a large, electrically operated machine having one large and one much smaller mesh drum. The larger drum contains 50,000 balls somewhat larger than marbles, which possess five-digit numbers matching those on the tickets sold. The small drum contains as many balls as there are prizes, and the numbers on these indicate the value of the prize.

Both drums are rotated the same number of times, and then one ball is released from each drum simultaneously. If the ball numbered 17187 drops from the large drum when ball Number 1 drops from the small drum, then Number 17187 wins the week's big prize, El Primero. The drawing is continued until all the balls have been drawn from the small drum.

On the Lotería's second floor, among the offices, is a kind of farmers' cooperative—a bank from which the *agentes,* the top class of licensed ticket sellers, can borrow money. They buy their tickets from the government, and often need money to tide them over until ticket sales pick up as the day of the drawing approaches. These loans are always repaid because, if not, the borrowers would immediately cease to be *agentes.*

NEW HAMPSHIRE STATE LOTTERY

In 1964, the State of New Hampshire broke a seventy-year precedent and became the first state since the abolishment of the Louisiana Lottery back in 1895 to operate a legal lottery in the United States. Until recently, tickets in the New Hampshire lottery could be purchased only from fifty-one state liquor stores, two racetracks, two toll stations, and from the lottery commission headquarters in Concord, the state capital. The New Hampshire legislature recently approved the sale of tickets in resort hotels, banks, fairs, and at public beaches, areas where out-of-state tourists are likely to visit.

The New Hampshire lottery is patterned after the Irish Hospital Sweepstakes. It combines a lottery with horse races. There are only two drawings a year, one in July, the other in September, both keyed to two horse races at Rockingham Park, New Hampshire. Recently the legislature moved to permit more drawings keyed to races at other tracks throughout the country when Rockingham is closed.

Tickets sell for $3. The purchaser writes down his name, and the tickets stay in the machine. The tickets are collected and placed in bank vaults and are taken out before the two horse races on which the sweepstakes are run.

All the tickets are mixed in a drum, and are then matched to 400-odd horses nominated for the races. Small prizes of $125 or slightly more are paid on the first matching. At post time, tickets matched to the entries in the two deciding races are paid some $3,000. The big prizes are two $50,000, two $25,000, and two $12,500 paid for win, place, and show in each of two races.

In addition there are monthly bonus prizes, totaling $5,000, that are designed to keep interest during the long period between drawings from September to July. These small prizes are based on computerized selections of numbers, and the winners get another crack at the next drawing.

The New Hampshire lottery gives back to the players 35 cents out of each dollar they invest. But New York State takes a bigger bite than that. It retains 70 cents of every dollar bet.

NEW YORK STATE LOTTERY

Tickets for the New York State lottery first went on sale on June 1, 1967, and the first drawing took place on July 20, 1967, giving New York State the distinction of being the second state in the country to get into the lottery business. The revenue is to be used to help educate the children of the State of New York. By law, New York State lottery tickets can be sold in banks, hotels, motels, and local government agencies. These total about 9,100; but at the time of writing, less than half, or about 4,000, are selling tickets.

The unattractive green-and-white tickets, which are stamped

Lottery Receipt, sell for $1. The purchaser writes down his name and address, keeps the carbon copy, and drops the original into a plastic box. Drawings take place once a month in Albany, the state capital.

In the monthly drawings, for each $1,000,000 in tickets sold there will be 15 winners in the grand-prize category, plus 225 consolation prizes. First grand prize is $100,000, second is $50,000, third is $25,000, and fourth is $10,000. The other 11 are $5,000 each.

Consolation prizes include 15 of $1,000 each, 15 of $700 each, 15 at $400, 15 at $250, and 165 at $150. It adds up to 240 winners, splitting up $300,000 in prizes for each $1,000,000 worth of tickets sold.

In addition to the monthly drawings, the New York State Lottery Commission proposes a $250,000 once-a-year free drawing to stimulate year-round ticket holders' interest in the state lottery. The payments to the winner of the $250,000 would be spread over a 10-year period to lessen the income-tax impact. This $25,000-a-year tax-burdened bonanza appears as a mere pittance when compared to Puerto Rico's $400,000 tax free semiannual top lottery prize.

Under the proposal, 200-odd tickets would be drawn and set aside from every one million tickets sold monthly, and put into a special drum. In addition to the top prize, there would be a number of consolation prizes ranging up to $7,500.

Like the Irish Hospital Sweepstakes, the New York State lottery is based on a combination of fishbowl-type drawings and the results of a horse race. But, unlike the Irish Hospital Sweepstakes, the New York State lottery is based on the results of a race run before the drawing takes place.

The reason given by various state officials for keying the top-money prizewinners on the results of a previously run race is to prevent the fixing of the race. Apparently some of New York State's officials don't think too much of the honesty of New York racing.

New York State's lottery gives back to the players 30 cents out of each dollar they invest, not such a good return when you consider that the Numbers game pays back 50 cents out of every dollar.

Lottery players, like all other gamblers, are a realistic lot; they care little who runs the game and to whom the profits go. All they are interested in is winning and collecting their reward. All other things are irrelevant.

The idea of raising money for education or other government needs through legal state lotteries is growing. A dozen other states are studying the example set by New Hampshire and New York.

Your Chances of Hitting the New York State Lottery

1 chance in 1,000,000 of winning the $100,000 grand prize
1 chance in 33,333 of winning $1,000 to $100,000
1 chance in 4,500 of winning $150 to $100,000

Why didn't New York and New Hampshire pattern their lotteries after the Puerto Rican lottery rather than the Irish Sweepstakes, one might ask? The answer is purely economic. These states wish to avoid the 10 percent Federal gambling tax, and since horse racing is the only form of legalized gambling exempt from this Federal tax, the drawings are keyed to horse races.

Despite the fact that the New York and New Hampshire lotteries do not give the player as good a break as the Puerto Rican and other government-sponsored lotteries abroad—they will go far, simply because "It's the only game in town."

If you were a New York City resident and breadwinner of a family of four with an annual income of $7,500 and purchased a New York State lottery ticket and were lucky enough to hit a million to one shot and win a $100,000 grand prize, you would be taxed $52,660.

First, the U.S. Internal Revenue Department would tap you for a lusty tax bite of $41,040. Next, the State of New York (which runs the lottery) would take a hefty tax cut of $9,760, and New York City would relieve you of another tax bite of

$1,860, leaving you $47,340. Nothing at present can be done to eliminate or reduce Uncle Sam's bite of $41,040, but New York State and New York City can do something about their tax bites. They certainly would be smart to eliminate the state and city tax and let the million to one shot winner collect an extra $11,620 for a grand total take home winnings of $58,960. An announcement to that effect would instantly increase the sale of lottery tickets.

Here are my recommendations to the New York State Lottery Commission that in my opinion would assure the state of a $200,000,000 revenue take.

1. Make the lottery receipt or ticket more attractive. At present it appears cheap-looking.

2. Revise the method of drawings. The final envelope drawing to determine the big winners of a race already run appears like a county-fair drawing for a door prize. In addition it appears to the ticket purchasers to be wide open for cheating.

3. Appoint ticket vendors to sell tickets where people work and congregate. All South American lotteries have ticket-vendor agents. The average lottery buyer dislikes going to a bank or hotel to purchase a lottery ticket. He likes to do it in secrecy.

4. Have the State of New York pay the federal, state, and city taxes on all top winners.

11

Betting on
the Horses

The findings of my recent women's race survey indicate that approximately 25 million Americans, of whom 11 million were women, made at least one $2 bet on a race during 1966—either with their favorite bookie or at one of the country's 150-odd thoroughbred or harness tracks. Of these 11 million women race bettors, 88 percent are housewives and salaried employees; 10 percent are businesswomen, professional women, or retired; 2 percent are gamblers, operators of gambling ventures, hustlers, and easy-money gals.

Twenty-five states have legalized the pari-mutuel betting system at the racetracks as a means of deriving income through taxation on each $2 bet made at the track. After the state and track have taken their percentage cut from the money wagered on each race, the remainder is distributed equally (on the basis of a $2 ticket) among those holding winning tickets.

It is a matter of record that a total of about $4 billion is annually bet within the confines of legal racetracks in this country. My sample findings indicate that about 25 percent, or $1 billion of these $4 billion, is wagered by members of the weaker sex—and it is common knowledge that many times that amount is bet illegally with thousands of bookies who accept bets by telephone or word of mouth.

A great majority of women race bettors, if pinned down and forced to tell the truth, the whole truth, and nothing but the truth, would admit that they know very little about horses, racing, or the theoretical factors required for the programming of races and the assignment of weights. The net result of this condition is to throw a substantial majority of women bettors on the mercy of those who claim to know what racing is all about. Following is a description of the various types of races and the present betting system used at thoroughbred and harness tracks throughout the country.

Maiden Race: Horses entered in a maiden race are those that have never previously won a race. In racing lingo, a horse who wins for the first time has broken its maiden, and cannot again compete in a maiden race at any track.

Claiming Race: Each horse is entered at a certain claiming price, and any horseman may claim the horse after the race, provided he has deposited an amount equal to the claiming price with the racing secretary's office in advance of the race. If two or more horsemen put a claim on the same horse, they draw lots to decide the claim. In effect, the claiming price is an effective system of grading horses. An owner will not permit a horse he thinks is worth $10,000 in a $5,000 claiming race. The horse probably would be claimed for $5,000; and even if he won, his winning purse of possibly $1,500 would not make up the loss. As for betting, the odds on this superior horse would be very low, and a heavy bet by the owner would drive the odds still lower.

Optional Claiming Race: Some states permit claiming races in which the owner of a horse has the opportunity of protecting himself against losing it. He simply does not file a claim form for his horse with the racing secretary's office; this makes a claim of that horse ineffective. The claim price range is listed with the entries for the race.

Handicap Race: In this type of race, any owner paying the required entrance fee may run his horse. But to ensure a real contest, the track handicapper (usually the track secretary) assigns a certain weight for each horse to carry in the race, thus adjusting matters so that each horse, in the handicapper's opinion, has an equal chance to win. He assigns the heaviest weight to the horse he thinks has the best chance, the lightest weight to the horse with the poorest chance, and other weights to the in-between horses in such a way that, if his judgment were infallible, all the horses would finish in a dead heat. If the weight of a jockey and his gear total 108 pounds, and the weight assigned to his horse for this race is 113 pounds, 5 pounds of lead are inserted into the bag (saddlecloth) to make the prescribed weight. The carrying weights are listed with the entries.

Allowance Race: This is similar to a handicap race except that the amount of the weights to be carried by the horses are not assigned by the track handicapper; they are determined by the rules set down by track officials in the condition book. The allowances and conditions are listed with the entries for the race.

Stake Race: These races are for the better horses, and the purses and entrance fees are much higher than in other races. The weights carried by the horses are the same standard weights for age and sex. All three-year-old colts carry the same weight; all three-year-old fillies carry the same weight, and so on. The theory here is that since the owner has paid a high entrance fee, he is entitled to test his horse against the others without any assigned weight handicap. Small racetracks sometimes run stake races in the same manner as handicap races when they lack the better horses.

Match Race: This is usually a race between two of the country's outstanding thoroughbreds, and the conditions of the race are arranged by the owners and trainers. Usually "winner takes all," meaning that the purse (sometimes more than $100,-000) goes to the winning horse.

Since the totalizer at all recognized tracks has a maximum

of 12 keys connected to the tote board in midfield, only the names and information concerning 12 horses can be flashed on the tote board. But since there are often more than 12 entries in a race, the racing secretary of each track has the authority to group any 2 or more horses in excess of 11 into a field. If 17 horses are entered, 6 would be grouped as a field. The secretary groups each field with horses he believes have the poorest chance of winning. A player who bets on a horse in the field collects if any of the field horses win. Always check your program to see if your horse is entered as a field horse. Bettors who don't do this may see the number of some other horse on the tote board as the winner, think their horse has lost, and tear up their winning tickets.

Also check to see if your horse is part of an entry, because if any horse of the entry wins you also collect. Entries are two or more horses that have either the same owner or the same trainer. The racing secretary may reject or accept entries.

The present race betting system provides for bets being made on any horse in a race, such as: (*a*) to Win (to finish first); (*b*) to Place (to finish either first or second); (*c*) to Show (to finish either first, second, or third); (*d*) any combination of win, place, and show—which is referred to as "across the board"; or a combination of win and place. (*e*) Daily Double: The bettor selects the horses she thinks will win in the first and second races, and buys a ticket on her selection; if both finish first, she wins. (*f*) Quiniela: The bettor selects two horses in one race to finish first and second, without regard to the order in which they do so. (*g*) Twin Double: The bettor collects if the four horses she bet in the four stipulated races finish first. The players first make their selection for the first two stipulated races, usually sixth and seventh races. If they both win, this ticket is "live," and is exchanged for another ticket bearing her selections for the third and fourth stipulated races, usually the eighth and ninth races. (*h*) Optional Twin Double: This is a variation of the Twin Double which gives the owner of a "live" ticket (winner of the first two stipulated races) the option to cash the ticket for its value at that time or to exchange it for a ticket on the regular Twin Double basis. (*i*) Perfecta or Exacta: The bettor picks one horse for first and another for second. If they finish exactly that way, she wins her bet. But if her choice for first comes second, and her second choice comes first, she loses. Owing to recent scandals arising from the nonpayment of federal taxes by many Twin Double winners, most racetracks in the United States have abolished the Twin Double.

Racetrack betting procedure is simple enough, but many women race bettors know almost as little about the betting system as they do about horses or racing. At Belmont Park one day, after the fifth race, I saw a woman tear up her tote ticket as she said to a friend: "Grace, I'm the unluckiest person in the world. When I bet a horse to place, it wins. If I bet it to show, it places or wins."

I picked up the torn halves of the ticket, looked at them, and returned them to the woman. "This is a winning ticket," I said.

"It couldn't be," she said. "I played the horse to place, and it came in first." When I explained that a ticket to place collects when the horse comes in either first or second, and a show ticket collects when the horse comes in first, second, or third, she groaned. "I've been tearing up winning tickets ever since I started coming to racetracks."

This woman isn't unusual; there are thousands of male and female bettors in the same boat. Many bettors throw away tickets as soon as they see that their horse did not finish in the money (first, second, or third). They don't realize that the horse that ran fourth, or even fifth, may pay off if it is later announced that one or more of the first three horses were disqualified. The State of New York has had as many as a quarter of a million dollars in uncashed valid tote tickets in one year. At least an equal amount must be picked up by stoopers, or ticket pickers, who make a practice of hunting for discarded winning tickets, which they cash at the windows.

Track bettors who can't recognize a winning ticket when it stares them in the face pay untold millions of dollars a year for their ignorance. They are, in effect, making a gift to the state treasury, which is hardly the horse bettors' favorite charity.

The majority of women race bettors are students neither of racing nor of betting. They go to the tracks for recreation and to satisfy their gambling urge. Most of them bet a couple of bucks on each race and on the daily double. Their methods of selecting horses are primitive. They pick horses because of some emotional association with the name of the horse or jockey or because of the colors of the jockey's silks. They like the way the horse switches his tail on the way to the starting gate or they have a psychic hunch, usually having to do with numbers. The occasional woman race bettor is almost always a hunch player.

I know one woman who won several hundred dollars on a 50-to-1 shot because a flock of birds flew over the track and she counted them and chose the jockey whose number matched.

The biggest daily-double payoff in history was won on July 4, 1954, by a San Diego widow, Mrs. Ottillia Alexander, who held the only daily-double ticket on Slick Trick and Rocklite at Agua Caliente. It paid $12,724.80. When reporters asked her how she had picked the two winning horses, she said: "It was easy. The post positions of the two horses were the same as the first two digits of my home street address."

Although most women are hunch players, there are many women who believe themselves to be handicappers. Their calculations, however, seldom give very many of them the same answer. Actually, their calculations are minimal; most of them follow very simple systems. Some are chalk players (who bet only on favorites); others bet only on long shots; others only on second- or third-choice horses. Some bet only on a horse who won his last race. Some bet only front-running horses, others on strong finishers. There are almost as many such systems as there are women form players.

The lady who really tries to select her horses on the basis of studying form finds that there is too much information available in the innumerable racing and scratch sheets, and much of it is contradictory. Even the professional male handicapper, skilled as he may be, has a real job on his hands. These experienced men spend considerable time every day studying the past-performance sheets of one or more daily racing papers. To them each race is a complex problem involving the mathematics of odds, furlongs, fractional times, track conditions, ages of horses, past performance, weights carried, post positions, and a dozen other contributing factors.

No matter how carefully they have weighed and divided and multiplied and compared these factors, Fate still deals most of the cards. Once the bell clangs and the horses spring from the barrier anything can happen—an unruly horse, a bad start, interference, a jockey's mismanagement of distance, a horse's nervous reaction. These unpredictable factors often make the best male handicappers look pretty silly. A number of years ago, at Saratoga, the favorites picked by these professionals lost twenty-two successive races!

Throughout an entire year I followed the best racing selection of three of the nation's outstanding handicappers. One lost 10 percent of his yearly gross betting handle; another, 12 percent; and the third, 14 percent—an average loss of 12 percent. And this is far better than the loss suffered by the average woman hunch player. Lady, it boils down to this: Even if you become a form player of professional caliber, the best you can expect to do in the long run is cut down your yearly losses.

However, it should be borne in mind that journalistic handicapping or selection of probable winners is legitimate compared to the "touting" racket. The tout (also called "tipster" or "chiseler") is a person who pretends to know which horse is going to win a given race and who for a fee will share his worthless information with any sucker who goes for the bait.

Although touting is not supposed to be permitted at the track, it is almost impossible to stop this petty-larcenous evil of racing. Lady, steer clear of any bearer of Greek gifts at the racetrack, especially if the bearer offers a tip on a horse.

Some of these information-loaded chiselers charge a fixed fee for their worthless information; others ask you to place a bet for them on their horse (using your money, of course). A tout may be anyone—a gambler, bookie, horseplayer, small horse owner, ex-jockey, stablehand, racetrack employee, former horse trainer, or the wife or girl friend of any of these. You may even be touted by one of your own friends who is innocently passing on a tout's tip.

Female touts usually team up with a man who poses as a husband or boyfriend. Here is one routine used by an attractive, good-looking couple in their middle thirties who usually work Aqueduct. They are adept at making friends rapidly with nearly anyone. Their angle for clipping the suckers is good; it can take several chumps at once.

The wife—let's call her Peggy—excitedly offers the information to likely prospects that she and her husband, Joe, have a confidential tip on a horse in the next race that they just received from a trainer. She is sorry she can't name the horse because the tip cost $50, and if too many players bet on the horse the odds will drop.

Just before the race is run, Joe fades, leaving Peggy with the marks (suckers, chumps). As soon as the horses cross the finish line, Peggy screams, "We got him! We got him!" And she names the winner. A few minutes later Joe reappears, counting a fat handful of bills. "Honey," he says, "we just won seven hundred bucks!" The marks are impressed.

A race or two later the same thing happens again. This is usually sufficient, and the marks are ready to spring (put up some money). Again Joe wanders off, and when he returns he says glumly: "He has a terrific horse in the next race, but he's asking $100, money in hand, before he'll talk. Do you think we should go for a hundred?"

This is Peggy's cue. She turns to her new-found companions. "There are five of us here," she says brightly. "If we each put up $20 we can all share in the winner." She makes it sound as though she were doing them a big favor. Since they have been praying for a break like this, it's in the bag. They put up $20 apiece, and Joe goes to buy the information. He comes back with the name of a horse, which he has probably selected by closing his eyes and poking a finger at the program. Everybody except Joe and Peggy, who haven't made even a $2 bet all day, gets some money down on the horse. If the nag loses, Peggy and Joe alibi the loss and lose themselves in the crowd. If the horse wins, they try to hustle a bonus from the winners. They usually succeed because the suckers figure they have a real good thing, and they want to keep Peggy and Joe happy so they'll share the tips they get the next day.

The touting racket is much more vicious away from the track because the chiselers don't have to worry about being spotted by track detectives or cops, and can use a greater variety of techniques. They run newspaper ads, contact players by phone or letter, send telegrams to prospective suckers, fake long-distance calls, and make use of stooges who pretend to have won big on the tout's tips. Touts often manufacture sucker bait by sending themselves telegrams signed with the name of a prominent horse owner or jockey, and giving the names of winners. The wires, of course, are sent after the races, with the times of sending erased or changed.

It's generally overlooked by women that you can't beat the races, because your winnings on a horse that wins, places, or shows are watered down drastically by all sorts of deductions and taxes. For example, at New York tracks, immediately after the betting windows close on a race, 11 percent of the money you wagered is assigned immediately to state taxes; another 4 percent goes to the track operators, for a combined total of 15 percent. The total cut deducted by the pari-mutuel system of betting in the 25 states where track betting is permitted is never less than 12 percent; the average is 15 percent, and goes as high as 20 percent. In Canada, Puerto Rico, and Latin American countries, however, the deductions run from 22 percent to 43 percent!

The money to be returned to winners is also reduced by the elimination of cents above the last dime, called "breakage," and adds about 2 percent to the authorized state and track deduction. This extra tax is imposed on the bland assumption that winners do not want to be bothered with pennies and nickels; but the fact is that it amounts to untold millions of dollars a year extracted from the race goer, and goes not only to states and tracks but also to your local bookie.

The simplest example I can give follows: Suppose $100,000

was bet on all the horses in the win (straight) pool and the combined state and track's mutuel take is 15 percent; then $85,-000 should be available to the winning players of that race, but it isn't. Suppose there are 8,957 outstanding $2 "win" tickets on the winning horse. Dividing $85,000 by 8,957 gives each $2 win ticket a payoff of $9.49, but the track rounds this figure to $9.40. Thus the state (or track) gets an additional "take" of $806.13 from the winning players. Place and show prices are computed the same way, but there is a difference, since two horses share in the place pool (the horses that ran first and second) and three horses share in the show pool (the horses that ran first, second, and third).

Nearly all women race bettors believe that the legal state and track take (15 percent plus 2 percent breakage in New York) is the only handicap they must overcome to have a winning day at the races. This is true if the lady bets on only one horse in one race; but when she and other bettors rebet winnings and the nonwinners bet fresh money, the 17 percent handicap jumps to 34 percent or more for nine races. For example: A crowd at a New York track that bets $200,000 on the first race will bet at least $2 million on the nine daily races. The state and track's take, including breakage, will be $340,000. The same 17 percent again. But we know that a racetrack crowd usually turns its money over at least twice in a nine-race card. A racetrack attendance that bets $2 million usually has only $1 million in its pocket prior to the first race. It achieves this magical feat by "re-betting the winnings"; that is, while the losers continue to bet fresh money out of their pockets, the winners, on the theory that this is their lucky day and that they are betting with the track's money, usually increase the size of their bets, and bet many times the sum they brought with them to the track. On average, each dollar brought to the track is bet twice, and since each time it is bet it suffers the 17 percent bite, the average bite is 34 percent of the money risked at the track. Thus, out of the race crowd's original stake of $1,000,000, it gets back only $660,000.

Lady, if you still don't believe that pari-mutuel betting is a sure way to lose money in the long run, let me try further to convince you with this hypothetical case. Suppose a factory owner who employs 1,000 workers wants to give them a day's outing at a New York racetrack. Suppose the track owners allow them the exclusive use of the track for that day, and suppose they can bet odd change. The benevolent factory owner gives each employee $10 on the condition that he bets the entire amount in the first race on any horse he likes and in any manner (win, place, or show).

It is also stipulated that the 1,000 bettors are to be partners, dividing their winnings and sharing their losses after each race. The winners always turn their winnings back to the factory owner, and he redivides the money equally among all the bettors. He wants everybody to have a good time. They all agree, and it sounds like fun.

They're off! Everybody has her $10 riding in the first race. After the finish the winners turn their tickets in to the factory owner, who cashes them and finds that, after the 15 percent state and track cut plus 2 percent breakage has been deducted, he has $8,300. He redivides this sum, and each of the 1,000 employees has $8.30 to bet on the second race. The winning tickets this time total $6,889, and when this is redivided each employee gets $6.88. This betting and redividing procedure is continued through all nine races. After the ninth race and the final redivision, each happy employee finds that his original $10 has shrunk to $1.86.

The state and track cut has taken $8,140 in legal deductions from the original $10,000. If the track had run 18 races, each player would finally be left with a grand total of 35 cents. No comment needed.

The illegal off-track race bookie, not satisfied with the totalizer's big bite, takes an additional advantage by limiting the payoff prices on winning selections. Most bookies pay "30, 10, and 5." This means that the limit payoff is 30 to 1 on a win bet, 10 to 1 on a place bet, and 5 to 1 on a show bet. It makes no difference how much higher the track odds on a $2 payoff price may be—30, 10, and 5 are all the bookie will give you. These bookie payoff limits of 30, 10, and 5, or whatever they happen to be, cut down the players' winnings considerably. Suppose the results and the track payoff prices won by a long shot are as follows:

	Win	*Place*	*Show*
Teeko	$66.00	$26.40	$16.20
Moko		10.40	6.50
Scarney			5.60

If you placed your $2 bet on Teeko at the track to win, you collected $66.00. If you bet the $2 with an Eastern bookmaker, you would get only $62.00. For a $2 place bet on Teeko, the track payoff would be $26.40 against the bookmaker's $22.00. On a $2 show bet the track payoff would be $16.20 against the bookmaker's $12.00. On Moko and Scarney, both the track's and the bookmaker's payoff would be the same as indicated on the chart.

This proves that the bookie often takes a greater P.C. than the track. He says he is justified because he runs the risk of being arrested and jailed. Most bookmakers will pay you the track mutuel on winning long shots if you insure your bet by paying an additional 10 percent of the total bet.

At most thoroughbred racetracks only straight betting and betting the daily double are permitted at the pari-mutuel windows. The bookie has no such mechanical limitations; he will also handle parlays, round robins, "if" money bets, reverse and back-to-back bets and insurance bets. These are all bets that can result in very large winnings from very small stakes, and so are very tempting. But the chances against them are too great. I analyze these below. I don't consider the ability of the horses, but discuss merely the mathematical and deceptive aspects of these bets.

1. The Parlay: This involves betting two or more horses with one stake. The horses are in different races and may even be at different racetracks. There are win, place, and show parlays. To play a win two-horse parlay, the bettor picks two horses to win, Horse A in any race or on any track, and Horse B in any race or on any track except the race in which the first horse is entered. If either horse fails to win, the parlay is lost. If both horses win, the parlay is won. The same holds true for a place or show parlay.

One reason I consider the parlay to be a sucker bet is that I doubt that there is a horseplayer in the country so successful in picking winners that she is justified in trying to pick two winners at the same time. The more horses in the parlay, the more foolish the bet. Three-, four-, and five-horse parlays are simply ridiculous.

2. Round Robin: This involves the playing of all possible two-horse parlays on three or more horses. Thus, a three-horse round robin is three two-horse parlays, 1–2, 1–3, 2–3. A four-horse round robin is six two-horse parlays, each horse with each of the other three horses. If a parlay is foolish, this is more so.

3. "If" Money Bets: Here you place a fixed amount unconditionally on a horse, and then stipulate that if this horse wins, another fixed amount shall be wagered on another horse or horses. This type of bet, as in the case of parlays, round robins, and so on, is an attempt by the player to multiply the winnings of a small stake. Actually, you are simply making two bets instead of one, and giving the bookmaker more profit percentagewise.

4. Reverse and Back-to-Back: This is merely a double "if" bet, and the player must put up two cash bets on two horses instead of one. For example: A player wagers $2 on Horse A, then "ifs" $4 on Horse B, then wagers $2 on Horse B and "ifs" $4 on Horse A. You could call it two "if" bets in reverse. Again the bookmaker earns more, percentagewise, than on a single bet.

Although round robins and back-to-back bets give the bookie a greater P.C. than a straight win, place, or show bet, many bookies refuse to handle such bets because they prefer to limit a player's winnings and don't want to risk a big money payoff.

5. Daily Double: Since the daily double is the best bet at the racetrack because the daily double pool is a separate entity and the track and state percentage deductions are taken off the entire pool rather than from individual races, one would think that the bookies would pay bigger odds on a daily double than on a two-horse win parlay.

Most bookies know that the track and state take a smaller cut out of a daily double than a bookie gets from a two-horse win parlay. But they ignore this and, as a rule, establish a limit of 75 to 1 on daily doubles and only 50 to 1 on two-horse win parlays.

Bookies figure it this way: In a daily double, players must pick the winners in the first and second races at the same racetrack—races usually run by poor horses. In a two-horse parlay the player may pick two horses from any race at any racetrack, and thus has more chance to pick better horses. As you can see, bookies don't overlook anything in their favor. Taking all the above bookie wagers into consideration, the advantage retained by the average bookie for accepting your illegal race bet comes to about 20 percent. Betting a bookie over a long run is nearly the same as throwing your money away. After 200 bets your chance of being a few dollars ahead of your bookie is 1 to 600. No wonder race bettors die broke.

Since there are thousands of female race bookies doing business in the United States today, you might be interested in knowing how members of the fair sex become bookies. I've met at least a hundred bigtime women bookies; but let me tell you about the first one I met. The only name I knew her by was Cleo. She operated in a southern resort city and employed about twenty girl runners, mostly showgirls and waitresses. When I asked her how she became a bookie, I got this story:

"Several years ago I was working as a waitress in one of the top restaurants in town and, like the rest of the girls, I used to bet a few bucks each day on the horses. I was giving my horse bets to one of my customers, a guy named Charlie who was a bookmaker. I also got the other waitresses to give me their bets, and passed them on to him. I wasn't getting paid for picking up these other bets, but Charlie seemed to be a nice guy and almost always left me a two-dollar tip every day with his cup of coffee. So, you see, I didn't mind doing him a favor.

"Then one day Charlie didn't show, and I couldn't give him the girls' horse bets. When I got through work that afternoon, I went looking for him and couldn't find him. I was worried. I wondered what I should do with the money and betting slips I had collected. I was scared, too. What if the horses the girls bet on won and paid a big price? I couldn't pay off. And I was sure the girls wouldn't believe me if I told them the bookie had disappeared.

"Well, that night I listened to the race results on the radio and checked my slips. Out of the twenty horses the girls bet on, not one horse won. It was the first time I was happy that the girls lost. I had collected $180. Well, I just figured that if the girls had won I would have had to pay them, and since they lost, the money belonged to me.

"The next day I collected the bets again, and Charlie didn't come in again. As a matter of fact, he still hasn't showed up, and this happened five years ago. At the end of the first year I made a $10,000 profit just by collecting bets from the waitresses. So I decided to quit my job as a waitress and go into the bookie business, and here I am. Today I buy a new Cadillac every six months and have more money than I ever dreamed I would have, thanks to my Charlie, the bookmaker who never showed up."

Cleo's book (total sum wagered) is now one of the biggest books in this southern city, and averages about $25,000 a week. She employs about forty runners, mostly women. Hundreds of players have become bookmakers in much the same manner as Cleo did, and it's still as simple as that today. It wasn't quite that easy before the introduction of the pari-mutuel system of betting, when the bookie had to know how to make his own payoff prices before the race. But now anyone can become a bookmaker, provided she gets an okay from the local political or racket boss and is willing to run the risk of being arrested. All a woman needs is the okay to run, a few hundred dollars to start her book, a number of horse bettors, and an elementary knowledge of arithmetic.

My survey shows not only that there are at least 10,000

women bookies in business today but also that this figure is rapidly increasing. Widows of bookmakers who are used to the easy money often carry on the book when their husbands die.

These bookies all employ at least one runner who picks up the bets from the players, pays off the winners, and collects from the losers the following day. I estimate that in New York City there are hundreds of women who are part-time runners or agents. They are employed as waitresses, receptionists in office buildings, elevator operators, factory workers, salesladies, and so on. They simply collect bets from their co-workers and other horseplayers and telephone them in to the bookmakers. For this service, the runners receive 50 percent of the weekly profit made from the bets they call in. If the runner's total bets show a loss for the week, she receives nothing.

A retired bigtime male bookie recently told me and a friend of mine, a New Jersey restaurateur, Larry Klunck, that he paid a girl agent who was employed as a $75-a-week secretary the sum of $20,000 during one year's period just for calling in her boss's horse bets. Her boss is the owner of one of the nation's largest firms manufacturing men's clothing. This girl thought she was smart. She insisted on 10 percent of her boss's losses, which amounted to $200,000 in one year. "It was a good deal for the secretary," the bookie explained, "and as for me, well, I just wish I had had a couple of more 'smart' gals like that working for me. If she hadn't insisted on that 10 percent, she would have gotten the usual 50 percent and made $100,000 profit for the year!"

The most ingenious system for fleecing bookmakers that has come to my attention was employed by the Blondie Mob, so called because the members were five attractive-looking girls, all blondes, ranging in age from twenty-three to thirty-five. How much money these girls cheated smart race bookies out of is anybody's guess. Some gamblers place the figure at $1,000,000, others at $2,000,000. I know for sure that they fleeced one bookmaker out of $100,000.

As a gambling authority and consultant, I am sought after by law-enforcement agencies, governments where gambling is legal, private clubs and organizations, and individuals who have lost large sums of money and believe they have been cheated but don't know exactly how. My policy is not to accept assignments from gamblers who operate illegally, but I did accept this one because of its peculiar circumstances and the challenge it offered.

The incident goes back a number of years. I was in Los Angeles, having just returned from a tour of army camps in Alaska, where I had been lecturing to GI's. The telephone in my hotel room rang one day, and a voice said, "Mr. Scarne, my name is ⸺. I wonder if you are available to take on a gambling assignment?" (Let's call the man Mr. Quinn, since that wasn't his name.)

I told him I might be if the price was right and if it interested me. An hour later, I entered a penthouse apartment in one of Hollywood's most fashionable districts. A butler opened the door, and I followed him into the study where Mr. Quinn waited. I recognized him instantly as one of the top bookmakers on the West Coast. He was far more intelligent than most bookies. I guessed by some things he said that he had had an accountant's training but had realized that he could make more and easier money as a bookmaker.

"Scarne," he said, "I handle one of the biggest books on the West Coast. My daily handle is seldom less than $30,000, and I think I know the ins and outs of the business, but I have a question. Do you think it is possible for a woman horse bettor to be so lucky she can overcome a bookmaker's percentage and win $100,000 within a four-week period?"

"A woman horseplayer has beaten you for $100,000 in four weeks?"

"That's correct. After she won $50,000, I began to think that maybe it wasn't just luck. Maybe she's just plain smart and has some angle for beating the races that really works, and maybe not. I have a special room in this apartment, but only big bettors are ever invited into it—and the girl is one of them."

I followed him across the large living room and through a

door into a well-equipped bookmaking room. It had all the standard paraphernalia: an adding machine, betting slips, racing sheets, ledger, telephone, table, and several comfortable chairs. Quinn said: "This room is on the top floor of the building. It's air-conditioned and soundproof and has no windows. What's more, my players must arrive here before post time. After post time, no one is allowed off the elevator at this floor until after the last race. I don't see how anyone in this room can get any information from outside. The bettors are not permitted to make or receive phone calls while they are here, and the phone number is not listed. If Blondie is getting information, I want to know how."

I told Quinn that my policy is not to make investigations for gamblers or gambling casinos operating outside the law. "But," I said, "I'm as curious now as you are, so I'm going to try to find out what's happening. If Blondie is cheating, she may be the smartest cheater I've ever seen."

The next afternoon found me scanning a scratch sheet in Mr. Quinn's luxurious bookmaking parlor. Several of his big-time betting customers were there, including the smartly dressed and attractive Blondie. I could see at once that she didn't have a radio-receiving gimmick on her; the low-necked dress she wore was a tight fit, and no room to spare.

When the races were over, Blondie was a $2,000 winner. After she and the other bettors had gone, Mr. Quinn turned to me and asked, "Well, is she lucky or smart?"

I smiled. "She's smart. She's been past-posting you, and the guy who has been tipping her off is you!"

"Me?" he exclaimed. "That's impossible!"

"I don't think so. When Blondie gave you that $300 straight-win bet on High Noon in the third race at Hialeah Park, it was already a couple of minutes after post time."

"So what? I let my bettors put bets down a few minutes after post in this room all the time. As a matter of fact, I don't even bother to look at the clock. When I get the results of a race over the telephone from my main office, I stop taking bets, but not until then. How could she get the name of the winner in this soundproofed room? If a bomb exploded across the street, you couldn't hear it in here."

"Like this," I replied. "Blondie knew that the third race at Hialeah Park had been run, and she got a coded signal from a confederate on the outside—a confederate who relayed the dope through you. Her confederate is the person who called in the bet on Snow Shoes in the eighth race at Hialeah."

Mr. Quinn immediately turned to the table and scanned his ledger. "That was May, another blonde! But I still don't get the whole gimmick."

"May called in quite a number of bets, didn't she?"

"Yes, but what has the Snow Shoes bet in the eighth got to do with the bet on High Noon in the third race?"

"May is operating from a room that has a direct line from one of the wire services. She gets the results of the race a minute or so after the race is over. As soon as she knew High Noon had won the third race, she phoned and gave you a bet of 50, 20, and 10 on Snow Shoes in the eighth, and she asked you to repeat it, which you did. Blondie heard you say, 'You bet me 50, 20, and 10 on Snow Shoes in the eighth at Hialeah.' And Blondie simply added the first digits of the amount of the bet, got an answer of 8, and knew that the horse listed as Number 8 on her scratch sheet had won the third race. What is Number 8 on Blondie's and your scratch sheet?"

Quinn looked at it. "It's High Noon! O.K., that's it." *

I learned later from Quinn that there were five blondes in the mob and that before they took him, many of the other bookies in the Los Angeles area had gotten the same treatment.

I don't know what happened to the Blondie Mob; I do know that they had a real sweet gimmick, and worked it more expertly than any male mob of cheaters that has ever come to my attention.

Lady, it should be obvious by now that "beating the horses,"

---

* High Noon and Snow Shoes were not the actual names of the horses involved.

or rather beating the track or bookie's adverse odds, is an impossibility in the long run. If you are one of the millions of women who go to the tracks to bet the horses for fun, remember that you must pay for the privilege. How much you pay is entirely up to you. If you want to keep the price down to what you think the entertainment is worth and what you can afford, here is a good system: Before leaving home, decide how much you want to spend (bet), add the track admission price, the price of a program, an allowance for refreshments, and the price of your transportation. The total is your budget. Take this amount with you and no more, so that if you lose you won't be tempted to recoup your losses and lose more than you planned.

Then bet the favorite to show. Bet for *fun*. Forget about win and place bets. I don't say that this advice will win you any money, but it will cut down your losses.

I tell you never to bet with a bookmaker, but if you can't resist the urge, also add these rules:

1. Bet cash only, never on credit; the temptation to bet beyond your means in trying to recoup your losses is too difficult for most people to resist. Credit betting ruins more bettors than anything else. Remember that "money you don't have on you, you can't lose."

2. Bet on a horse running at a track where the state and track percentage cut is the smallest, because if you win, the mutuel payoff price will be more.

3. Make as few bets as possible so that the money wagered, if lost, won't disturb you mentally.

4. Bet your horse to show if you can. (Some bookies won't accept a show bet unless it is accompanied by a win or place bet of equal money.)

5. Stay away from parlays, "if" money, and back-to-back bets.

6. Always remember that when you picked a winner, you were lucky; it wasn't good handicapping. And don't forget that "You can beat a race, but not the races."

12

How to Win
at Gin Rummy

Lady, at the very outset, I make this promise: No matter how good a Gin player you are, the strategic tips, hints, warnings, and subterfuges that follow will help you to win many more Gin games than ever before. It is information that I've gathered over the years from the country's crack male Gin players. The analysis will center on Gin Rummy, but most of the counsel can be put to profitable use in any game of the Rummy family.

Watching thousands of male and female Rummy players, and tens of thousands of Gin games down through these past twenty-five years, I've made it my business to observe the small, fleeting mannerisms of winning and losing competitors, to cross-examine hundreds and hundreds of good and bad players, to measure the difference imposed on the play by the stakes of the game, and to observe not only that women do indeed bet considerable cash on a single game but also how they bet it.

Therefore I can tell you this: My observations of mixed (male and female) Gin Rummy games over the years have convinced me that Gin Rummy is still a man's game. By and large, I believe most women have a streak of curiosity that is too active for a Gin Rummy player. Most women, even the best Gin players, sometimes make a bad discard against all reason. This may be because many of them believe Gin Rummy is more a game of chance than of skill.

Let me dispel at once this misconception that "Gin Rummy is all luck": winning Gin requires greater skill than winning Bridge. Bridge is a partnership game, and as in all such games, one partner is usually more skilled than the other. Their combined ability is therefore less than that of the better player. In Gin Rummy, with each player usually on her own, a skilled player is not handicapped by a less able partner; her skill potential is not reduced. If you lose more often at Gin than not, it's because you are not so good as your opponent, not because of the "bad hands" you have been dealt.

Every male or woman Gin player who is a consistent winner has little tricks of his or her own. There are, in the mass, scores of such tricks, developed over the lives of these players by trial and error and by costly experience into a very substantial body of learning. No one player has mastered all of them. Perhaps no one player can. But I'm going to tell you about most of them, and we'll begin with the mechanical errors that take place in picking up the hand.

How to Avoid Mechanical Errors

Never pick up your original dealt cards at one time. It is impossible to impress them on the mind when they confront the eye in their natural confusion. Pick them up one at a time, sorting them as you go, impressing them on your mind, and marshaling them for your first play. Moving this deliberately, you can appraise the chances on every possible combination of your cards; and at the very least you have them in orderly array when the time comes for you to make your first play.

This is a prized secret among topnotch Gin Rummy players. More women make their worst play at the very start of a Gin hand than at any other time. I have been amazed at how many experienced women Gin players very often discard a useful card at the start because they failed to observe its connection with another. Don't forget: Pick up your Gin hand slowly, and arrange it carefully so that all combinations are evident at a glance.

When arranging cards in your hand, put together:

1. Your melds.

2. Your possible melds; that is, two cards of the same rank or of suit sequence.

3. Your unmatched cards according to suits.

Group your two-way combinations in some way, logical to you, so that they can be recognized easily. If you have the 6 of diamonds, 6 of spades, and 7 of spades, they should go together that way so that if another 6 or an end card of the spade sequence turns up, it will fit tidily into your holding. But—

4. Avoid having a regular high to low order for your ten cards. Don't put your high combinations on one end and your low ones on the other end. Keep combinations together; mix high and low combinations.

After having arranged your cards so as to impress them on your memory, you must now shift them around during play (just as all expert Gin players do during the play of the hand). Don't keep your melds or possible melds in the same position throughout the hand, for the simple reason that you may thereby give your opponent the same kind of information that you are attempting to gather from the way she plays and arranges her cards.

When to Take the Upcard

There is no need to debate taking the upcard when it fills in a meld. But when the upcard doesn't give you a meld, the decision to take or leave it poses a problem. In this connection, I am going to give several rules that will help you decide when to take and when not to take the upcard.

If the upcard is an ace, you should always take it unless you have a perfect gin hand and the ace is absolutely useless to you. If you hold a very weak combination hand and the upcard gives you a possible three- or four-way combination, by all means take it. Example: suppose the 3 of hearts is the upcard and it does not give you a meld. Does that mean that you should pass it without question? Not at all. It may be worth taking if it helps your hand even though it does not give you a meld. If you reduce your hand by getting rid of a useless high card, or if it gives you a likely combination—say you have the 4 of hearts and the 3 of clubs—it may be well worth while because it gives you four possible ways to form a meld; second, you have the extra advantage of deceiving or puzzling your opponent.

Are you losing a turn, giving up a chance to pick a really helpful card by taking a slightly helpful one? Not at all. You are only giving up half a chance. You have your choice of passing and not helping your hand at all or helping your hand a little, confusing your opponent a little, and also perhaps depriving her of a chance to improve her hand.

Remember, however, that when your opponent is first, she also may be taking the first card to deceive you.

Discarding

Early in the game, and whenever possible, it is advisable to discard a card ranking one or two away (preferably one away) and in a different suit from the one previously discarded by your opponent. Don't tell your friends; just remember this rule and watch the improvement in your game. For example: Your opponent's first discard is the 9 of clubs, which is probably a bait card. Hence, bait or no bait, your safest discard is either the 8 or 10 of diamonds, 8 or 10 of hearts, or 8 or 10 of spades, or the seven or jack in spades, hearts, or diamonds. If you do not hold such a card, your next best bet is to discard a card of rank equal to one that your opponent has previously discarded. There are only four possible ways in which an equal-rank card can be used against you. Any other

card can be used six ways in a meld. That is, unless you're holding stoppers—cards that will prevent a discard from being used
in a meld by your opponent.

But when throwing a discard of rank equal to one previously
discarded by your opponent, bear in mind that this may be
precisely what she wanted you to do. She may have thrown
the first as bait. She may want your card of equal rank but in
a different suit. All players use bait from time to time; it is
the job of the player to detect the bait and avoid the hook.

When you decide to break up a pair, and the other two cards
of the same rank are alive and perhaps in your opponent's
hand, don't talk about that. What she doesn't know can't hurt
you. And maybe she won't know unless you tell her.

When in doubt about her next discard, the average woman
Gin player will throw her highest unmatched card every time.
She thinks that at least she is reducing as many points as possible, and insists that she is playing it safe and smart. I want
to warn all women who fit this group that this habit is responsible for the loss of many a Gin game that otherwise would
have been won.

The only time it is advisable to discard the highest unmatched
card is when playing to the score; otherwise, pay no attention
to the amount of points your discard will reduce your hand.
When playing defensively, try to discard the card that is least
likely to help your opponent; when playing offensively, try to
discard the card that is least useful to you.

When to Knock

A decision you are very often called upon to make is whether
to knock or to continue on for Gin. There can be no definite
instruction at this point without ifs, ands, and buts. All things
being equal, it is best to go down as soon as you can. Don't
let the extra reward in points, in thrill, and in personal satisfaction, trap you into waiting for Gin when your knocking
hand is an almost certain winner. Here is a piece of advice

that I'm sure will reward you with countless additional winning hands. When in doubt whether to knock or to play on for Gin, by all means knock.

Playing the Score or Keeping Under

When your opponent's point total is close to game, you must be extra careful about the unmatched card point total in your hand. You must try to "keep under." That means that you must reduce your point total so that, if possible, even if she goes Gin her score will still be less than the total required to win the game. Short of that, try to get your total low enough so that a knock will not win the game for your opponent. I agree that there are times when it is a better bet to hold those two tens with the probability of getting the third one, than to discard them in favor of a 5 and a 6. But in most cases, if you are aware of the necessity for reduction, you will be able to discard high cards with safety equal to the discard of a low card. Also, there are times when your chances of getting low-card melds are just as good as your chances of high-card melds.

Just being aware of the necessity of keeping under will improve your winning chances by 25 to 33⅓ percent. Except for expert play, my observation is that every third or fourth final hand of the game between two women is lost because of the avoidable failure of one or the other to keep under.

Reading the Discards

Although it is my ruling, and the standard practice of the game, that discards cannot be spread and examined, nevertheless Gin experts glean a lot of forgotten lore from the discard pile.

The discard pile is seldom so perfectly squared up that a player cannot see a few cards whenever she really wants to.

And the information refreshed in your memory by a glance may be crucial to the development of the hand.

Before discarding, if you are the least bit doubtful about the play, go ahead and take a candid peek at the discard pile. Everyone else in the house is doing it. Don't be a chump.

An expert Las Vegas Gin player put it to me this way:

"Don't try to study the discards. Just try to form them in your mind into sequences. If you see a 10, a jack and a king of spades in the discard pile, you start thinking in terms of queens. All right; look again. You're looking now for any other queen. And if you don't see her in the discards, rest assured that the queens are alive and kicking."

When to Play for Gin

The only time to consider playing for Gin is when you believe that knock will be underknocked (undercut) or when you have four or more chances to go Gin. A live ace (or king) can be used four ways. A live 2 (or queen) can be used five ways. All other live cards (3, 4, 5, 6, 7, 8, 9, 10, and jack) can be used six ways.

The ideal Gin hand, of course, is one when you have nine ways to Gin—when you hold three three-card sequences that can be switched about to form three three-card melds of the same rank. This holding constitutes your maximum chance of a killing.

For example: You hold the 7, 8, and 9 of clubs, 7, 8, and 9 of diamonds, and 7, 8, and 9 of spades. These can be construed and used as three 7's, three 8's, and three 9's. And the player has nine chances of drawing a card to go Gin: three 6's, three 10's, and one each of 7, 8, and 9.

A five-card spread or two four-card spreads are of little or no help when going for Gin.

As a general rule, if you have four or more ways to go Gin—play for Gin. If you have three or less ways to go Gin—knock.

Final Gin Rummy Advice

Maybe the following won't sound cricket. Inquiry: What is ethical in Gin Rummy for cash? One male player in the Las

Vegas money crowd likes to arrange to stand behind any potential male opponent and size up his style of play. He wants to know whether the man is methodical, whether he speculates rashly or well, whether he favors a knock hand instead of going for Gin, whether he gets nervous under the baleful glare of a fistful of high cards, how he talks when the cards are running with him and when they're against him. Card players, like everyone else, tend to be creatures of habit. They react, often unconsciously but always eloquently, to their circumstances. Is it unethical to study those reactions? I hope not. I've been doing it most of my life. And I'll generalize about what I've seen:

Many players will clam up when they have a bad hand and talk it up when they catch a good one.

The vast majority of players are methodical, no matter how they try to mix up their styles. And method can be observed and learned.

The most dangerous player is the person who has mastered what I call the two-way hand: one that will enable you to go Gin with a pick of one or two cards or to knock with a pick of one or two others.

In conclusion, I wish to say that there are 15,820,024,220 possible ten-card hands in Gin Rummy; and because I won't be around to watch your game, I can't tell you what cards to hold or discard or when to knock or go for Gin.

But I can assure you of one thing. If you have seriously studied and faithfully applied the strategic information, hints, mathematics, and subterfuges given in the foregoing text, and you still lose to one special player, make it your business to study the chapter entitled "Protection Against Card Cheats." It will be time well spent.

Be suspicious.

Take precautions.

These rules can't cost you anything, but they will save you plenty.

13

How to Win
at Poker

My nationwide survey of card gambling in the United States shows an adult card-gambling population of 69 million, of whom 36 million are women and 33 million are men—a nationwide increase of 1 million women cardplayers and a drop of 3 million male cardplayers over the previous six years.

Poker (Stud, Draw, Deuces Wild, and so on), by far the most popular card game played in America for the past half-century, had more women devotees in 1966 than ever before— 26 million. Rummy (Gin Rummy, Canasta, Seven-Card Rummy, and so on) ran a strong second with 20 million women players, and Bridge was in the Number 3 spot with 11 million women adherents. Pinochle ran fourth with 2 million ladies, and Hearts, Pitch, and Cribbage ran a dead heat for fifth place, each favored by some million-odd women.

Most women questioned stated that they did not confine themselves to the one form of card playing they listed as their favorite, but also indulged in one or more cardplaying activities. Hence, the figures shown above include countless women who voted for two or more games.

With reference to all money wagered by women in private card games, Poker led with 55 percent. Rummy was second with 30 percent. The remaining 15 percent was wagered on all other forms of private card games, such as Pinochle, Hearts, Pitch, Cribbage, Bridge and so on. Bridge generally, unlike other games discussed herein, is played primarily for enjoyment; stakes, if any, are usually small.

Before 1930, or thereabouts, Poker was almost exclusively a man's game. Today the weaker sex, with its 26 million Poker adherents, outnumber male Poker players by 3 million. Every day millions of women now gamble with each other in thousands of private homes and at women's Poker clubs, and more millions gamble with men every day in the tens of thousands of mixed Poker games. The reason for this drastic drop in male Poker playing in America lies in the stepped-up police raids (Federal, state, and local) on clubs and private homes where men are suspected of illegal cardplaying. Most law-enforcement agencies think twice before raiding an all-women's Poker, Rummy, or Bridge game. As far as I know, in the past several years only three illegally operated all-women's card games were raided by police in the United States. When we compare this to the hundreds of police raids conducted weekly all over the country on various card or Poker clubs patronized by men only, we can readily understand why more women play cards than men.

Only two states, Nevada and California, permit commercialized cardplaying. Nevada's casino-licensing law permits all-out Poker, Blackjack, Faro, and Rummy (Pan) playing. The California law considers Closed, or Draw, Poker to be a game of skill and Stud Poker a game of chance; towns may, by local option, issue licenses for Draw Poker to Poker clubs. Gardena, the most famous of these California towns, has seven big Poker palaces, each of which has the legal maximum of 35 Poker tables.

The fact that cardplaying can be played commercially in only two states, and the fact that private cardplaying for money is not permitted by law in any state, are examples of how unrealistic and outdated our gambling laws are.

Illegal though it may be, 26 million women do gamble at Poker in private clubs and in homes in every city and hamlet from the Atlantic to the Pacific and from the Canadian border to the Mexican border.

At least a hundred variations of Poker are being played today, but all can be placed in two large classes: Closed, or Draw, Poker, in which each player's cards are hidden from the other players until the showdown or the completion of the hand; and Open, or Stud, Poker, in which some cards in each player's hand are exposed to all the players as the betting progresses.

To most women, Draw Poker means the game of Five-Card Draw—jacks or better, and its popular variations: Low Ball, Draw Poker—Blind Openers, High-Low Poker, and so on. Stud Poker usually means Five-Card Stud and its variations: Canadian Stud, Seven-Card Stud, Six-Card Stud, Low-Hand Stud, High-Low Stud Poker, and so on. These variations, and many others, are played in various combinations: Table Stakes, Freeze-Out, Deuces Wild, Joker Wild, Dealer's Choice, Jackpots, and so on.

Every one of America's 26 million women Poker players can't be a winning player, but I know that a poor Poker player who makes use of the information I am about to present can become at the very least an average player. And the average-or-better player will surely improve her game.

Space does not permit reprinting the complete up-to-date official rules of Poker contained in *Scarne On Cards;* for a thorough study of the up-to-date rules of all card games you should obtain a copy. If you don't know the proper rules of Poker, you won't be able to take advantage of the finer points of the game.

Because Poker has so many playing variations, and because the strategy varies with the style of game played because of the differences in rules, it is difficult to formulate a precise overall strategy that will be applicable to every situation that develops at Poker. However, after studying the most common faults committed by most women Poker players I have succeeded in formulating a body of general-strategy rules, hints, tips, and warnings that apply to all forms of Poker and that are planned to correct these faults and help to make you a winning player, or at the least save you considerable money.

If you play cards in any professional Poker game, whether in a swank home on Fifth Avenue that caters to women only or with the boys and girls in one of the licensed Poker clubs of California or Nevada, you must pay for your Poker seat. Running a professional card game is a business, and a charge is always made. How much you pay depends upon the place; and the kind of Poker game you choose is entirely up to you.

In the licensed Poker clubs of California and Nevada, the operators charge a fee for playing on an hourly basis, usually running from a low 60 cents per person at a 25-cent limit game to a high of $5 in a really big-limit game. This is reasonable enough, for it pays the operator's overhead, salaries, taxes, and so on, and earns him a profit. Since Poker gets a lot of play, it is sometimes quite a lot of profit: one of the larger Gardena Poker palaces grosses about $15,000 a week, or nearly $800,000 a year, which is not peanuts.

But if you are one of the millions of Poker players who patronize games in which the operator takes 5 percent of the money in each pot for herself, you are paying a lot more than you may think.

For every licensed Poker game in America, there are thousands and thousands of illegal Poker games patronized by women. Many are friendly weekly games that rotate from one player's home to another's. Others are illegal house games run as a business. In many illegal games the operator's take (her or his charge for furnishing the gaming facilities) is a 5 percent cut taken from each pot.

If this doesn't sound like much of a charge, would it surprise you to learn that even the world's best Poker player, playing against rank suckers, would eventually go broke bucking that small 5 percent cut? The operator calls it 5 percent, but it is actually much greater, often as much as 10 percent. In most professional games the operators get a percentage, or cut, of the players' winnings; but Poker, like pari-mutuel race betting, is one of the few games in which a charge is also taken from the winning player's bet.

An example: Four women play an entire Poker hand to the showdown; the pot totals $40, and the house takes a 5 percent cut, or $2, out of the pot. The winner of the pot has paid a cut not only on her winnings but also on the $10 she put into the pot. The operator is really taking a cut of 6⅔ percent on that player's $30 winnings.

Or suppose two women play a Poker hand to the showdown; the pot totals $40. The 5 percent cut gets the operator $2, as in the four-handed game, but from the winning player's standpoint this is 10 percent of the $20 she won.

A while back I clocked 40 different mixed Stud and Draw Poker games (women and men) for a period of 3 months. The maximum betting limits ranged from a low $1 to a high of $20. When I averaged my figures I found that:

1. It takes about 2 minutes to play an average hand.

2. In an average Stud game approximately 30 hands are dealt per hour.

3. The average pot in a 6-handed $4-limit game contains about $30 on the showdown.

Now let's see how strong this 5 percent cut can be in the average game. Thirty $30 pots per hour means that the operator's 5 percent cut gets her $45 per hour. In a Poker session lasting six hours, the operator takes a total of $270.

Let's assume that each lady began with $50 and that she received the number of good, bad, and indifferent hands that probability says she can expect in the long run. The total money the players invested at the game's start was $300. The total cut is $270. That small 5 percent cut has accumulated to 90 percent of the starting stake.

Never having stopped to dope this out, there are millions of women Poker players who try to win under these conditions. Many of them play two or three nights a week without the slightest realization of the enormous price they are paying for the privilege of letting the operator get most of the money.

And, believe it or not, many women Poker-game operators aren't satisfied with the way that 5 percent cut earns them money. They often steal extra amounts from the pot. This is usually done when making change or taking out the cut. The player who wins the pot is so pleased at winning that she seldom notices that the cut has been taken, let alone spotting the theft.

It is difficult to understand the logic, if any, of Poker-game operators. If they charged a reasonable hourly rate, as is done in the legalized games of Nevada and California, they would have a Poker game most of the time. As it is, they break most of the players in a few weeks and then wonder why they no longer have a game.

Many women Poker players who have gone broke time and time again stay away for a while as they try to figure out why. Most attribute their losses to bad luck. Few think they were cheated, which is possible. But more often it's the 5 percent cut that did the trick. Not knowing the real reason, these women eventually come back and try again to buck the impossible.

Some operators charge a 2 percent or 3 percent cut, which eats up your bankroll just as the 5 percent charge does, except that it takes about twice as long to do the trick.

Lady, if you play in such a game after reading the above analysis of the 2 percent, 3 percent, or 5 percent house cut, and still think you can hope to come out ahead in the long run, don't say I didn't warn you.

If the Poker game is honest, and the cut or playing charge is small or nonexistent, and you still lose consistently, what is the reason? It's a simple one. A steady winner plays better than her opponent; a steady loser plays worse. Here's the way I put it in one of my early gambling-lecture demonstrations at a women's club when a lady said: "I have been a steady loser at Poker since the first day I joined this club. Is there any advice you can give to help me win at our next Poker session?"

"Yes," I told her. "There is one big secret, a Poker policy that, if put to use, will not only make you a winner at your next session but at most of them. It's a policy that is practiced religiously by the country's best male Poker players. It is the only surefire rule that wins the money, and it's simple: Don't sit in a Poker game with superior players. If you have been losing consistently in the club's weekly games, it's a cinch the girls you've been playing with are better players. Find another game. Find one in which the players are softies (poor players). Poker is the world's greatest skill or money-management game, and an inexperienced player who knows too little about it hasn't the ghost of a chance against seasoned players."

I gave her that advice many years ago. It is just as true today. You may object that Poker is not so much fun when playing against poor players. I agree. An even better policy is to study the game and improve your skill so that you can win even among good players. In short, don't just read and forget the hints, tips, and rules for winning play that follow here; study them, remember them, and put them into practice.

To play winning Poker, the most important thing to remember is to be alert. Every little movement has a meaning all its own. Every draw, every card shown has a vital bearing on your possibilities of winning the pot. Therefore, you must watch every player in the game to see that you are not being cheated or chiseled; you must watch every active player so that you can gauge the strength of her hand, so that you can judge her reactions to a raise or reraise, to a draw of two cards or three cards, and so on. In Stud Poker especially, you must observe each player's upcard carefully to see what it does not only to your own chances for improving your hand but also to the betterment or detriment of the chances of every other player, as well as the player who received the card. Finally, you have to watch yourself, to see that you don't betray your hand, to see that you don't give clues to your opponents. You have to be alert.

And you can't be alert if you're overtired or mentally disturbed by something either in the game or apart from the game. And you can't be alert if you're drinking or have been drinking. Don't play Poker for sizable stakes if you've had a tough day cleaning the house, if you're worried about money, or if you're troubled about Junior's grades.

To play winning Poker you must be keen at all times; you must be fast and able to size up all situations at a glance. If you do that, you have a good chance of winning, even if you are just an average player. For there will always be one or more players who, because of fatigue, irritation, recklessness, or fuzziness, will play badly and give you the edge.

If it's for fun, and the stakes are unimportant, and you don't care whether or not you win, do what you like. But if you want to win, remember that the first rule is: Be on your toes; be alert at all times.

Whether the game is Stud, Draw Poker, Low Ball, Seven-Card or Five-Card, Deuces Wild or Nothing Wild, there are ten important Scarne winning rules of play to remember. If you remember these rules, it is almost impossible for you to lose in an evening of Poker unless you are playing with a group of experts who also know them. If you play Poker regularly with the same group of players, and find that there are a few people who win consistently while the rest of you lose, leaving the possibility of dishonesty aside, it is because these players are aware of these rules and play according to them.

SCARNE'S TEN RULES FOR PLAYING WINNING POKER

The first rule: Learn the correct rules of the game so that in case of an argument you can protect your money. Often a bad decision against a player has broken her for the evening. If you know the rules, no smart-aleck will be able to cheat you of a pot by a bad decision. Learning the house rules of Poker in the game you patronize is easy enough. Simply ask the operator before sitting down to play. A player familiar with the rules enjoys a considerable advantage over one who is not.

The second rule: As I said before, if you are a neophyte

Poker player, don't get into a game in which the players are old hands. Experience is a big factor in Poker; it is very hard to overcome with mere talent. If you are lucky in a game with such players, you win little; if unlucky, you lose heavily. Try to find a game where the players are no better than you.

The third rule: Keep a poker face. Don't complain when losing or show elation when winning. The emotional aftermath will prohibit clear thinking and proper evaluation of your hand. Don't indulge in unnecessary conversation. Keeping a poker face means keeping the same disposition at all times. Such restraints are very difficult to acquire overnight, but they are essential requirements of a good Poker player. Not only will you play your best game; it will also be difficult for your opponents to figure out your hand.

The fourth rule: When you have nothing, get out. More money is lost by the Stud Poker player who goes in with two indifferent cards and drops out later, or by the Draw Poker player who stays with a low pair and folds after the draw, than is ever lost by having three kings beaten by three aces, and so on. The player who has the patience to stay out of pot after pot is the player who, in the long run, will win. However, to try to camouflage that obvious give-away habit of playing them tight or back to back, you should occasionally play with nothing, that is, if the price you pay is not too high.

The fifth rule: When you're beaten, get out. You may have a pair of queens back to back in a Stud game, a high hand, good enough to win ninety-nine pots out of a hundred. But if on the next card one of your opponents should show a pair of kings or aces, in most cases the smart play is to drop out at once. You may improve your hand, but the chances are you won't. And even if you should improve, your opponent may improve also, and his pair was better than yours to begin with. Except for going in on nothing, more money is lost by trying to beat a high pair with a lower one than anything else in Poker.

The sixth rule: When you have the best hand, make them pay. If you have a pair of aces back to back, make it as expensive as possible for your opponent with the pair of queens to play. It is true that every once in a while you will be outdrawn, but you will win much more often, and you can afford your opponent an occasional victory.

The seventh rule: Forget friendship. Upon entering a Poker game, leave friendship behind. If you hold a "cinch hand" at Draw or Stud, and allow your friend to see your hand without making her pay to call your hand, I can assure you that you will not be a winner. Poker is a game for blood. If you want to play a good game, you must forget friendship and bet your hand for what it is worth. Top money winners do. You must. Trust no one at Poker.

The eighth rule: Don't attempt to bluff a pot when four or five players are still in the game, or keep raising before you have your complete hand, with the thought in mind that you are going to win with a bluff. The legends of money won by bluffing at Poker are greatly exaggerated. Seldom do good Poker players attempt to bluff, because as a rule they are not in the pot at the showdown with a weak hand. The best time a bluff should be attempted is when one or two players are in the pot—and they are heavy losers. If they are heavy winners, don't attempt to bluff, because, ninety-nine to one, you will be called. Don't try a bluff on a beginning player, because as a rule she will call. The really good Poker player can be bluffed more easily than the beginner.

The only time the bluff is an important factor in a Poker game is in a high-stakes game, where a player may bet $20 or more on a bluff hand to win a $10 pot. But when a pot totals $20 and the maximum limit is $2, and you were not the opener or high hand, you will be called at least twenty-four times to one.

Never attempt a bluff at Stud unless you have a little something in your hand. When playing Draw Poker you must start the bluff by raising before the draw to attempt to impress on the other players that you have a strong hand.

Should you get caught bluffing twice, it's about time for you to stop for that evening. It is too costly to attempt bluffing after being burned once or twice. Not ever to attempt to bluff, however, would mean a considerable loss of call money on the showdown, once you became known as a player who never bluffs. The other players would hesitate to call you when you do bet.

It is a good practice not to show a hand after a successful bluff, unless you do not intend to bluff for the remainder of the Poker session. And if a player does not call on the showdown, bluff or no bluff, don't show your hand. This merely serves to give the other players more information concerning your playing methods.

The ninth rule: When you have a good hand, don't be too anxious to put your money into the pot until it is your proper turn; don't even have your bet ready. Untoward eagerness will inform your opponents, before they need know, that you intend to play. Most beginners or poor Poker players are very anxious to bet on a good hand, and, conversely, when holding a weak hand, to turn down their cards before their turn of play.

Don't try to win a small pot with a big bet. For example: A player makes a 50-cent bet at Stud Poker, holding the high card; another player raises the bet $2 for a total of $2.50 in the pot. The player with the high hand drops out; the player who raised wins the 50 cents with a lower hand than the player who dropped out had. That is not considered a bluff. Such a player may win a few half-dollars, but she will eventually lose many times more on one hand when she raises that $2 and finds that one of her opponents has that high pair backed up. In short, don't try to win small amounts with a big bet. It doesn't pay off.

The tenth rule: Do not lend money to another player in a Poker game. The money you lend will often help to break you. And, as a rule, it is an even bet you will never get it back. Gambling debts aren't paid back as often as legitimate debts.

If studied seriously and applied faithfully, the above tips, hints, warnings, and rules of strategy must make any alert woman a winner at Poker . . . providing she is not being cheated. If you play Poker in a joint that operates outside the law, and if you lose and lose and keep losing against all probabilities, your Poker-playing opponents may have something more than skill working for them. Some card cheat or card mob (group of cheats) may be taking you to the cleaners. To protect yourself against such distasteful characters, I recommend that you study the next chapter, "Protection Against Card Cheats."

14

Protection Against
Card Cheats

Though I should have preferred sparing you the reading of this chapter, we had better face the facts about playing cards for money. And one of these facts is that more cheating takes place at illegally operated private card games patronized by women and men combined than at all other forms of gambling. The main reason, of course, is that the average woman knows little or nothing about card-cheating techniques, and hence is more easily victimized than men.

In a private, illegally operated Poker, Rummy, Pinochle, Blackjack, or any other big-money card game patronized by women and men, the chance is 1 out of 5 that a male card cheat is at work. Even Bridge tournaments, where only cardplaying prestige is at stake, are infested with bridge cheats. Thousands of Bridge tournaments are played annually throughout the world; few, if any, are completed without one or more incidents in which a team appeals to the tournament directors for redress from some unfair practice committed by an opposing team. And much more cheating goes undetected by the players. I know because I have seen it.

Of the 200 all-women's Poker and Rummy games that my female aides scouted during my gambling survey, we found that cheating in one form or another took place in 1 out of every 10 games. My female helpers detected 5 decks of marked cards in use and saw cheating in one form or another taking place in 15 other games. Most of these women cheats spotted in action were very amateurish in their methods. And it was sometimes very difficult for my helpers to distinguish between the amateur woman cheat and the thoroughgoing, no-holds-barred, but honest woman player.

Now, what constitutes a cheater at cards? I myself am sometimes, after all these years and experiences, perplexed about a player: Should he or she go into my book as a scoundrel or as just a thoroughgoing, no-holds-barred good player? When I was a young man I used to play Gin Rummy with an elderly lady, a business acquaintance of mine, who might be characterized as straddling this borderline. She had a habit, after the cards had been cut for her to deal, of peeking at the bottom card in squaring the pack. She's looking at a card that will never get into the play of the hand. Harmless? Ye-e-es. But her very knowledge that this card is dead gave her a measurable percentage of advantage over me in planning the play. She has seized relevant evidence that was not available to me. She was a cheat!

And she is the most dangerous kind of cheat, the amateur kind. For the amateur cheat is generally your friend. You are not going to mistrust her. You are not on your guard. So the amount of money that you lose—you collectively, all you good-natured American women suckers—runs into an aggregate of millions of dollars each year.

For every dozen crooked moves made by the agate-eyed professional, the amateur cheat will attempt blandly and brazenly innumerable swindles:

1. The amateur cheat in Gin Rummy will attempt to lay off on a meld a card that doesn't belong in that meld or will dis-

card two cards instead of one or will call his or her count for the scoresheet an amount less than it actually is.

2. The amateur Stud Poker cheat will just forget to ante up, and then will swear earnestly that someone else is shy.

3. The amateur cheat in Canasta will fabricate 30 or 40 points on the count of the hand. Trapped in a recount—any embarrassment? Not a bit! We're all entitled to a certain percentage of error, aren't we?

4. Finding the dealer panicky or busy, the amateur cheat at Draw or Stud Poker will announce she is changing a $5 bill in the pot, takes an extra 50 cents out of the pot, and considers the feat an act of skill. It never even pinks her conscience!

In the following text I'm going to refer to the most common methods of cheating at cards, but first let me advise you what to do when you suspect someone of cheating:

Never accuse any person, particularly a friend, of cheating. It is highly possible that an honest player may do, quite unconsciously, some of the things that cheaters do. You have no right, and there is no need, to raise a hue and cry. The application and enforcement, quietly and graciously, of the rules of the game in progress will remedy whatever's wrong or looks wrong. If that doesn't help, you can stop playing then and there, quietly and graciously. No offense, no harm done, to anyone's sensibilities or reputation—or to your pocketbook.

Rules are made to be followed—or broken revealingly—by players. A lady friend told me once: "John, I play with a good friend of mine. She never offers me the cards for the cut. I'm afraid to insist on the cut; she may think I'm accusing her, and I value our good relations. What should I do?"

I asked her who was the winner between them, and she said her friend was about $100 ahead.

"I don't know whether your game is lousy or you're being cheated," I told her. "I've never seen you play. But this I do know: If you were cutting the cards, you would not be suspicious of your friend. That's a lot worse than losing $100."

You must decide such things for yourself. As for me, I play

by the rules—I stopped playing with the old lady who peeked at the bottom card.

There is, however, one unsuspecting amateur cheat you may never catch at her work against you, the cheat you never escape, the lady card shuffler, the person who loves you most—yourself. You'll never be a winning card player unless you stop cheating yourself while shuffling the cards.

At least 95 percent of women card shufflers that I've watched during my lifetime do not know how to shuffle a pack of cards correctly. And the lack of this card-shuffling ability costs them untold millions of dollars annually. There are numerous advantages that you give an opponent when you shuffle incompetently. Lady, if you've been using the overhand shuffle, which is the very mere matter of sliding cards in blocks of two, three, four, or ten from one hand to the other, mixing them grossly, then you must give up that shuffle immediately. The cards just can't be mixed thoroughly that way. Groups of cards will stick together. Try it right now. Assemble a deck in groups; give it an overhand shuffle; then turn the spread deck face up on the table. You find (don't you?) that at least one group remains as you put it together.

Cheaters—and locaters (honest, hard-driving money cardplayers) too—know this about the overhand shuffle, and take advantage of it. Here's how!

In the previous Gin Rummy hand you held four kings. The inexpert woman dealer picks up the cards, leaving the four-king meld intact, and gives the cards a single overhand shuffle, nonchalantly letting them flop from the upper hand into the lower. The observant opponent, watchful as a cat, notices where the kings lodge in the reassembled pack (that's easy enough!), and gets ready for the kill.

The kings were near the top of the pack in the pickup. The single overhand shuffle puts them close to the bottom. Your opponent cuts the pack a little below its center, say two-thirds of the way down. Now, if the game is two-handed, say Gin Rummy, ten cards are dealt each player alternately.

Each player gets a pair of kings. The locater knows you have a pair. You don't know she has one. It is quite an advantage for her.

Or one of the kings is lost in the shuffle. The locater gets only one king. But she holds it, and your chances of forming a king meld are reduced 50 percent.

Or you catch three of the kings and the locater gets the fourth; she knows that by holding it she'll be able to lay it off on your meld.

Or the locater catches the three kings and you get the fourth. As a rule you discard it at your first opportunity, giving your opponent a four-card meld.

And the locater's knowing which king you hold will always enable her to avoid discards that would build up a sequence meld in your hand.

Next we have the lady riffle shuffler show-off. She cuts the deck into two nearly equal packets, holding each lengthwise in each hand. She riffles both packets together, and then takes special pains to interlace the edges of both packets together. She then lifts both hands, holding the cards in a viselike grip from the table. She then applies pressure on both ends of the packets of cards, forcing them to bend upward; then she re-leases them and applies a downward thumb pressure on the uppermost bent cards, and you hear the riffling noise when the cards shuffle together. I agree that it looks great and impresses your opponent with your card-shuffling skill . . . but it also gives your opponent a good look at the cards as they riffle to-gether—something the lady card shuffler show-off fails to see, since she's at the wrong angle and is busy impressing her op-ponent with her fancy riffle shuffle. As a rule, the observant opponent often spots the five or six bottom cards.

There are numerous advantages, then, that you give to an opponent or opponents when you shuffle cards incompetently. The only defense against bad shuffling is to make use of the table riffle shuffle as employed by professional card dealers the world over.

And even the riffle shuffle is susceptible to abuse, especially by women. Most women cardplayers learn the principle, but then shuffle the cards so carelessly that the bottom four or five cards of the pack are not disturbed, or go through the shuffle in unchanged order. See—now, with a deck—whether you are one of these soft-touch shufflers. If you are, change your habits immediately, because the locater's accurate knowledge of what those cards are and how they'll fall gives her an insuperable advantage over a long session at any game.

And—again with a deck—see whether you are one of the many amateurs who shuffle the cards at such an angle to the horizontal that their opponents can see the cards as they click into position. Always hold the pack close to and flat against the table in shuffling; to correct your angle, practice shuffling in front of a mirror. The mirror will show you everything your opponent can see as you handle the cards. Pretty revealing, isn't it?

At least 50 percent of all women card shufflers make this mistake after a shuffle: They take the pack up into their hands to square it before offering it for the cut.

Why, after taking such pains to conceal the bottom card, must they thus expose it to a hawk-eyed opponent? Because— make no mistake about it—a sharp opponent will take advantage of that card. She'll know where it is after the cut. She can cut the pack in such a way as to force it into the deal (placing it high in the pack) or keep it out. In either case, a significant percentage swings in her favor. Square the cards flat against the table.

It must be a matter of record that I'm a card manipulator by trade. I know how to shuffle, and I'm going to take the liberty of assuming you'd like to be taught by a professional. Nothing fancy about it; it won't take much time; and, while I don't guarantee to transform you into an expert card manipulator, I think that the next five minutes we spend together will save you money and insure you against ever being embarrassed by shuffling badly.

THE SCARNE SHUFFLE

First, place the deck flat on the table directly in front of you. Grab the deck on the extreme ends with both hands, thumbs and fingers opposite each other, tips resting on the table (see Figure 1). Pull about half the cards off the top of the deck with your right hand while holding the bottom half with your left hand. Then place the top half flat on the table end to end with the bottom half.

Second (Figure 2), let go of both halves and shift your left- and right-hand grips to the two packet ends nearest each other and riffle the halves together by running your thumbs up the sides of each half.

Third, after the cards have been riffled together, release your hold, and with the palm of each hand slide them into a single block by bringing your palms toward each other, as in Figure 3. Never take the cards off the table, either for the riffle or in the act of squaring the pack.

Fourth, get into the habit of cutting the cards just for insurance at least once during the shuffle by pulling out the bottom half and slapping it onto the top between riffles—good protection against locaters.

The GI's of World War II used to call this the Scarne shuffle. It's foolproof, crookproof, and as slick as a hustler's coiffure . . . and it'll save you money if you never play anything but Solitaire. It even saves wear and tear on a pack of playing cards.

A couple of last warnings against your most insidious enemy:

You're not playing for paid admissions; so you don't have to expose yourself to kibitzers. If you can do so without awkwardness, try to sit with your back to a wall so as to cut down your audience. Many a hand is betrayed to an opponent by a spectator's sigh or chuckle or sharp inhalation of breath or some foolish remark such as, "What a hand!"

Before each game—whether Stud, Draw, Gin, Pinochle, Bridge, Hearts, Pitch, or any other game—do yourself the justice of checking the deck, just to be sure the whole pack's there and nothing is missing or duplicated by any accident.

The Scarne Shuffle

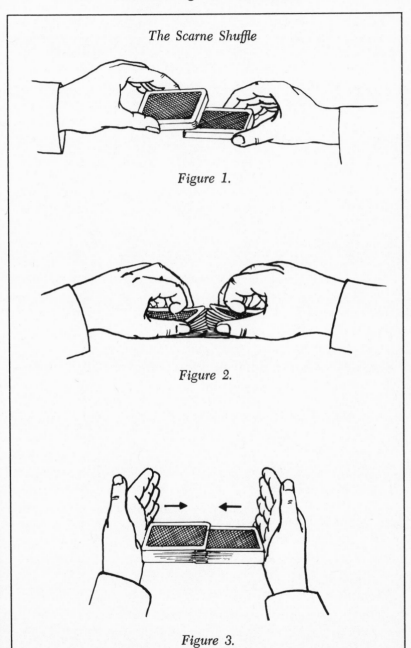

Figure 1.

Figure 2.

Figure 3.

And don't play when you're disturbed. Most of us are convinced we play a pretty good in-and-out game; we tend to be champs one day and chumps the next; and we attribute it all to the run of the cards.

Malarkey! Irregularity in quality of play at the amateur woman's level is strictly a matter of mental attitude.

When you play cards, give the game all you've got or get out. Not only is that the one way on earth to win at cards; it's the only way you and the rest of the players can get any fun at all out of what ought to be fun.

You can't play a poor hand well if your mind's on the children or your husband's ulcers or your friend's operation. When you don't remember the last upcard your opponent picked, and you throw her the like-ranked card that puts her Gin, or when you call an opponent's cinch Poker hand, it's time to push back your chair and say, "Girls, I just remembered I have a previous engagement."

Do as most male professionals do. When they make a few bad plays in a row, they just mutter, "That's all for today, gents," and they mean it. They mean that today is written off; they mean they'll be back tomorrow, which is another day.

By all means, when you're in this kind of losing streak, don't let yourself get panicky. The more reckless you feel, the more desperate is the necessity that you get away from that table at once. An excited player, a player plunging to recoup losses, is a player at her worst.

Learn to recognize her. That player has been and will be—unless you learn how to deal with her—your own worst enemy.

And one more thing: The player who resorts to cardplaying systems is just adding method to her madness; she is systematically insuring her losses. There is no such animal as an unbeatable card system. Only the inexperienced woman cardplayer believes in one.

The next thing a woman money cardplayer should learn is to protect her money against card hustlers and cheaters. If you can't do that, you'd better stop playing cards for money right now. Take time out to read about cheating and how to protect yourself against card cheaters. One second of sleep in a fast Poker or Rummy game might break you for that session and plenty of others. Among other things, it will pay you to keep your eyes on the discards. Many women and men card hustlers will reach for a valuable card for use in her hand. When you catch her, she is kidding; when you don't, she takes your money.

The most common cheating technique or device used to fleece unsuspecting cardplayers is the marked deck. About 1 out of every 200 (or 330,000 of the 66,000,000) decks of playing cards sold annually in this country are marked at some time or other so that some or all of the 52 cards may be read from the back. Marked cards are the most widely used mechanical cheating device, and are employed by many women cheats because they require no manipulative skill, are surefire money winners, and are almost never detected by the average, easy-going, unsuspicious woman cardplayer.

My survey results show that not more than one average woman card player out of five hundred knows how or where to look for the markings. Not long ago, I gave a card-gambling lecture demonstration for a women's club, and during my demonstration I tried an experiment. I handed a dozen women each an unopened pack of playing cards with the simple statement, "These packs—four Bridge, four Poker, and four Pinochle —are marked decks. See if any one of you ladies can spot the markings. I'll give each of you one hour to find the marks." This was a challenge the twelve women couldn't resist, and they went to work to prove that they could spot marked cards when they saw them. Like almost everyone else, they had heard of marked cards. The decks looked exactly like others they had purchased innumerable times at their local drugstore. Satisfied that outwardly the decks were no different from the others, they broke the stamp sealing the case. After taking the decks from the cases, they examined the glassine paper in which the cards were wrapped. They found nothing. Then they tore off the paper and began examining the backs of each card in the deck. It was an arduous task, but all of the women stuck to it for a full hour. At the end of the hour, each of the twelve women had to admit that she couldn't spot a marked deck, even after having been told the decks were marked. I spent the next half hour reading the backs of cards of all twelve decks, while the assembled women guests kept shaking their heads.

These twelve women, like millions of others, didn't know where to look because they did not know the principles of marking, which are usually the same on all marked decks. The moral of this story is that you'll be smart to stay out of any fair-sized money card game until you learn how to spot marked cards.

The user of marked cards does not have to be a sharp gambler, nor does she (or he) have to practice daily to become a card expert. All she needs, besides larceny in her heart, is the knowledge of where to get a deck of these ready-to-use marked cards, from a friendly male gambler or from a novelty or "magic supply" store. Any idiot can walk into a magic-supply store, plunk down $3 or so, and receive a deck of marked cards with instructions on how to read the backs. However, the printed instructions carry a notation that these cards are to be used for amusement purposes only. Thereafter, when you sit in a "sociable" game with this cheat, you're the idiot, because she can read the backs of the cards as easily as if the faces were exposed.

Though you buy the deck yourself from a retailer you know and trust, it may be marked. During one festive racing season when gambling was wide open in Saratoga, every deck of cards sold in town was marked. A mob had moved in and switched a case of marked cards in place of a case of cards just shipped by a big legitimate distributor. The marked cards were duly retailed. No matter where a player bought a pack of cards during that racing season, they bore the mob's markings. I have been told, almost reverently, that what happened after that was pretty impressive.

The average woman has several misconceptions about marked cards. She believes the cards are marked when they are printed. They aren't; reputable card manufacturers abstain from such chicanery. But, some of their cards are marked later. Some small-time card-supply-house owner who is interested in an extra buck, or the cheat himself, buys honest decks of standard brands. They heat and soften the adhesive and remove both the sealing stamp and the glassine wrapping. Then the cards are marked by hand with special matching inks. Finally, the glassine wrapper is replaced and neatly repasted; the deck is reinserted in its case, and the stamp is glued on again. It's as simple as that.

Although individual marking systems vary, most card markings fall into two kinds: "light and heavy." If the cheat has what she (or he) believes to be smart and alert opponents, she purchases a deck with light markings. Light markings are a finer mark, and impose more eyestrain on the user. If the cheat sizes up the opponents as suckers, the heavy marking is used. Most cheats use heavy markings when the opponents are all women. Generally, heavy markings can be read across the average card table, a distance of three or four feet, by anyone with normal eyesight who knows what to look for. More ink is used; that's all.

Cards are invariably marked along opposite edges, either horizontally or vertically, so that the cheater can read an exposed edge regardless of the position of the top card of the deck, or a card resting face down on the table or a card in the hand.

THE SCARNE RIFFLE

To detect marked cards, use the Scarne Riffle Test. It is a marked-card detection method based on the principle of animated-cartoon books, with which you may have played when you were a child. When you hold such a book firmly in one hand, and riffle the pages rapidly with the fingers of the other hand, the figures printed on the pages seemed to move. It's the principle on which the motion picture is based. Try it on the cards you suspect may be marked. Hold the cards in your left hand face downward. Hold your left thumb firmly over the center of the back of the top card. Now, pull back the narrow edge of the deck furthermost from your body with the fingers of your right hand and riffle them rapidly, keeping your eyes on the back of the design (see Figure 4). An honest design will stand utterly still. If the cards are marked, a shifting of lines will appear on the backs. When this occurs, note the exact spot where the shift took place, and compare it with the like spot on other cards. If they vary, they're marked.

There is only one rule I can give you as an overall tip for spotting marked-card cheats. Watch the guy or gal who keeps his or her eyes glued to the backs of cards—cards that are about to be dealt, the hole card in Stud, the top card of the deck in Gin Rummy, the important card in any game.

The gambling world has many names for various types of sleight-of-hand card cheats. In the western part of the United States, Nevada included, a professional card cheat who travels over the country seeking card games where he can ply his trade is called a "crossroader." A cheat who specializes in palming cards is referred to in the trade as a "hand-mucker" or "holdout artist"; one who deals from the bottom of the deck is a "base dealer" or "subway dealer."

The surreptitious manipulation of cards by card cheats, hand-muckers, holdout men, crossroaders, card sharks, base dealers, or other card cheats requires considerable skill and practice, plus the nerve of a thief. A top-notch card cheat who is intent on beating casinos must be considerably more adept with a deck of cards than a first-rate magician. The magician is free to use a great deal of conversation and misdirection to fool his audience, but the card cheat is limited by the game's regulations. In all my gambling experiences I have met only three women who rated as skilled cardsharps. One was a former Nevada Blackjack dealer, another a former lady magician, and the other a former operator of a Chicago cardroom.

I must make it understood, however, that male and female card cheats who specialize in fleecing women cardplayers do not fall into this select group of skilled manipulators. They are a breed of inept card bunglers and crooks, and the only reason they exist is that the average woman cardplayer is still a babe

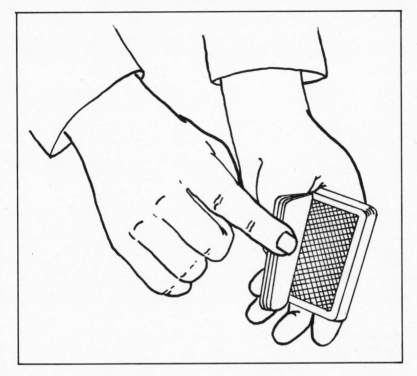

Figure 4. The Scarne Riffle

in the woods and can't bring herself to believe that people she knows and plays cards with would cheat.

The ruses and subterfuges used by these distasteful crooks are so many and varied that a detailed description would more than fill this book (see *Scarne on Cards* and *Scarne's Complete Guide to Gambling*). The knowledge of how these crooks operate, and the ability to take countermeasures, will serve to safeguard the observant woman cardplayer.

Most card thieves announce the fact that they are cheats long before they make a crooked move. They do so as soon as they begin to deal. The giveaway is the peculiar manner in which they hold the deck, known as the Mechanic's Grip (see Figure 5).

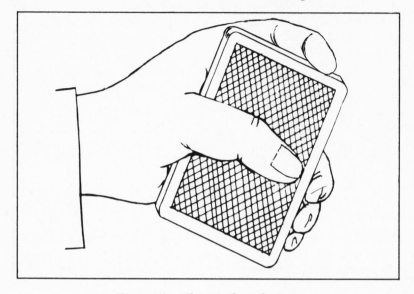

Figure 5.   The Mechanic's Grip

The cheat holds the deck either in the right hand or in the left hand (we shall assume from here on that it's the left hand). Three fingers are on the edge of the long side of the deck, with the index finger at the outer-right corner. Some card cheats keep two fingers on the side of the deck and two at the outer corner.

Many professional dealers in gambling casinos also hold the deck in this manner, but for a different reason: They do so to prevent players from glimpsing the' bottom card. But when you spot a player using the Mechanic's Grip in a private friendly game, find yourself another game. The odds are that the player who holds the deck this way is doing so because peeking at the top card, second dealing, bottom dealing, and other cheating moves require this grip. The index-finger position at the outer corner of the deck acts as a stop when the cheat is second dealing and peeking, and also helps conceal a card when it comes from the bottom of the deck. It is possible that an honest, even innocent, player might accidentally hold the deck this way, but it is highly unlikely because it takes practice to hold the cards in this manner while dealing. The only reason anyone would practice this grip is that he intends to cheat. There's one exception: Magicians also use the Mechanic's Grip, but (like myself) not many of them play cards for money, for the same reason I always give: "If I win I'm accused of cheating; if I lose, they think I'm a lousy magician."

THE SCARNE CUT

There's a good defense against the skilled or clumsy card cheat who employs sleight-of-hand or subterfuge to stack the deck and deal himself or his confederates the winning hand. It's the "Scarne Cut," a cut I invented during World War II as a defense against cheating for men in the Armed Forces. The Scarne Cut is accomplished as follows when the cards are offered to be cut:

1. Pull a group of cards from the center of the deck and place them on top of the deck.

2. Square up the deck of cards; then repeat the above procedure again, and, if desired, a third time.

3. Square up the deck of cards and cut the deck in the regulation manner, simply by cutting a group of cards off the top of the deck.

The drawings (Figure 6) show the Scarne Cut in action.

The use of this cut eliminates in one stroke most of the cardsharp's best cheating moves. Use it and you won't need to worry about most of the card cheats' crooked techniques—such as bottom deals, stacked decks, crooked shuffles, and crooked cuts. At the very least, it will give any cheat enough headaches to cut his (or her) cheating close to the vanishing point. It may frighten him (or her) out of the game entirely or even into playing honestly.

After you have convinced yourself that you have been victimized in a card game—then what? That's hard to answer. It depends on the place and the circumstances—but be very careful.

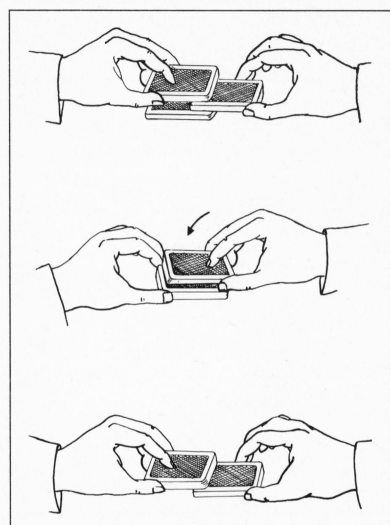

Figure 6.   The Scarne Cut

1. *Pull a block of cards from the center of the pack.*
2. *Place them on top of the deck and square it up.*
3. *Pull a block of cards from the bottom of the pack, and place them on top.*
4. *Repeat steps 1, 2, and 3 again—several times, if you wish.*
5. *Finally, square up the pack and cut it in the regular manner.*

My advice is to forget all about it and stop playing—because, as I have learned over the years, cheating is difficult to prove; furthermore, any cheat caught red-handed (or simply accused) is dangerous. Move with caution.

One last tip: If you're suspicious, get out of the game.